CHRISTMAS CRAFTS

CHRISTMAS CRAFTS

*Festive projects for making
decorations, gifts, cards and treats*

ALAN D. GEAR AND BARRY L. FREESTONE

COLLINS & BROWN

This edition published in Great Britain
in 2005 by BCA by arrangment with
Collins & Brown
The Chrysalis Building
Bramley Road
London W10 6SP

An imprint of **Chrysalis** Books Group plc

1 3 5 7 9 8 6 4 2

British Library Cataloguing-in-
Publication Data:
A catalogue record for this book is
available from the British Library.

ISBN 1 84340 322 6

Designer: Elizabeth Healey
Project editor: Miranda Sessions
Commissioning editor: Marie Clayton

Reproduction by Classicscan, Singapore
Printed and bound by Imago, Thailand

Contents

Introduction

One of the most fabulous things about Christmas is that it offers a wonderful opportunity for using all your craft skills to the full – as well as a being a great time to try out something a little bit different. During our 25 years of working in the crafts arena we have met hundreds of interesting and enthusiastic crafters and in this book we have collected together some of our very favourite ideas for the Christmas season. Here you will find the very best projects to decorate the home and tree, ideas for making your own cards and giftwrap, as well as festive food ideas to welcome your guests. As you plan and prepare for the festive season, consult this book for exciting ideas and information to guide you on your way and make this important holiday time really special for everyone.

In the first chapter we cover different ways to make your home look really festive and welcoming. Here we have some traditional projects, such as the Holly and Ivy Garland, but also some contemporary projects; the beautiful Beaded Rainbow Catcher will look stylish and modern wherever you hang it. Chapter Two looks at projects to decorate the tree – so why not try out the

sumptuous braided baubles, or the pretty felt birds. Of course, one of the central parts of Christmas is giving gifts to our relatives and friends to let them know how much we have appreciated them over the year. Chapter Three shows you how to make really personal gift tags and cards and Chapter Four has a selection of delicious food gift ideas, including mouthwatering biscuits and chocolate treats.

Most of the projects featured in the book use seasonal materials and simple techniques, so no matter if you are a novice at craft or a seasoned professional, you will find something inside to try. Everything is clearly explained, with a list of the materials you will need, detailed instructions and step-by-step photographs, as well as lavish photography of the finished item.

Packed with festive and creative ideas, *Christmas Crafts* is the definitive guide to creating the perfect Christmas. Let us show you how to make your Christmas really special this year.

Alan D. Gear and Barry L. Freestone

Decorating *the* Home

Gourd Fairy Lights

YOU WILL NEED

*Dried gourds
(1 for each fairy light)*

Metallic paints

Paintbrushes

Scrap piece of card

Bradawl

Plastic card

Scissors

A string of outdoor fairy lights

Epoxy resin

Outdoor fairy lights really do create an enchanting atmosphere for Hallowe'en parties or to decorate a tree close to the house. Bell cups are small dried gourds that are sold for use in dried flower arrangements, usually fixed to sticks which are easily removed. They can be found in either a pale natural wood colour or sometimes dyed in bright or deep colours. As well as being useful for floral displays, they make colourful covers for fairy lights. Painting the insides of the cups in bright metallic colours will add an iridescent shimmer when the lights are switched on.

1 Make sure that the insides of the gourds are clean and dust-free. Paint the insides of each gourd with metallic paint, alternating the colours and leave to dry.

2 Place the gourd on a piece of card to protect the work surface and make a hole in the base of each gourd with a bradawl. Start by piercing the woody base from the right side and enlarge the hole bit by bit. The hole needs to be just big enough for the light bulb to go through.

3 Cut a pair of 4.5cm (1¾in) circles out of plastic card for every light. Make a hole in the centre of one card circle just big enough for the wire flex to go through. Make a larger hole in the second circle, big enough to fit around the base of a light. Cut through each circle from the outside edge to the central hole and snip out small 'V' shapes around the outside. Pull a light bulb through the hole in the gourd base and place the circle with the larger hole around the base of the light. Apply glue to the underside of the circle and stick in place inside the gourd, pulling the light and flex back into the cup.

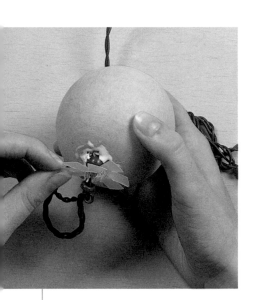

4 Place the second circle with the
   smaller hole around the flex at the
outer base of the gourd and glue in place
to secure the light inside. Fix the other
lights in place inside the gourds in the
same way.

Gilded Candlestick

YOU WILL NEED

Large wooden candlestick

White wood primer

Paintbrush

Pale pink water-based paint

Very fine sandpaper

Jar of copper coloured gilt cream

2 soft rags

This elegant, tall wooden candlestick has been decorated using an unusual technique. Instead of using gold leaf, the metal (in this instance, copper) has been mixed into a wax base to produce a fine powder. This makes it a particularly suitable method for gilding complicated surfaces such as the turned candlestick shown here or moulded picture frames. It is an ideal project for transforming a tired and familiar household object.

1 If the candlestick is not already primed, apply the white primer and allow to dry thoroughly. Next, apply two coats of pale pink paint and allow to dry. At this stage, you can sand the surface with very fine sandpaper to obtain a smooth finish, if you wish.

2 Apply the gilt cream to a rag and gently rub into the surface with a circular motion. Don't apply too much at a time as you need to obtain a broken finish where you can see the base colour through the gilt cream. Apply solid copper on the flat circular sections of the turned design. When the gilding has been completed, leave the candlestick for 15 minutes, then rub the surface very firmly all over with the clean rag until it shines.

Copper Candle Sconce

YOU WILL NEED

★

*Roll of soft copper foil
0.1mm (4/1000in) thick,
16.5cm (6½in) wide*

★

*Tracing paper template
(see page 148)*

★

Invisible tape

★

Dry ballpoint pen

★

Small, pointed scissors

★

Piece of card

★

Sewing tracing wheel

★

Bradawl

★

Hole punch

★

Aluminium can

★

Strong scissors

★

Protective gloves

★

3 brass paper fasteners

Many people would never dream that they possess the skills necessary to work with different metals. However, they are really very simple to learn – no special techniques are required and some everyday tools have been adapted. This decoration looks stunning placed on a mantelpiece.

1 Cut a piece of copper foil 20 x 16.5cm (8 x 6½in) and lay the tracing paper template on top. Stick in place with invisible tape and draw over the lines with the dry ballpoint pen, pressing very lightly onto the foil beneath to transfer the outline and design. You will need to place the foil on a piece of card or a pile of tissue paper – this provides a yielding surface and protects the worktop.

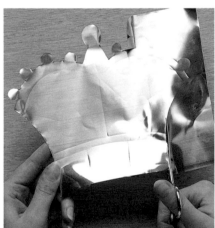

2 Remove the template to reveal the faint impression of the design. Use the small, pointed scissors to cut carefully around the outline, paying particular attention to the small bobbles along the top.

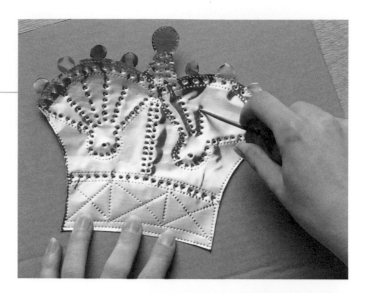

3 Place the crown shape on the card or tissue. Roll the tracing wheel firmly over the transferred lines, add more decoration at this point if you like, then pierce through the copper from the front with the bradawl.

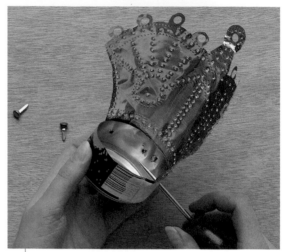

4 Next, using the hole punch, make the larger holes in the bobbles along the top of the crown. You will need to press the handles of the punch together very firmly to produce a neat hole with clean edges.

5 Cut down an aluminium can leaving 3.5cm (1⅜in) upstanding from the base. This is easily done with strong scissors, but you may wish to wear gloves to protect your hands from any sharp edges. Wrap the copper crown around the aluminium can base and, using the bradawl, pierce three holes through both metals.

6 Push each paper fastener through these holes and open out the two arms behind the crown and inside the can, making sure they are pushed firmly back, allowing the crown to stand upright.

Honesty Wreath

Make a welcome change from the rather over-used dark green ivy or holly and predictable red berries by creating this ethereal wintry wreath in palest green and silver to grace your front door.

This unusual and magical combination uses the papery seed heads of honesty and silver thistles which grow so abundantly in the Swiss Alps, opening in dry weather and closing slightly when the air becomes damp like little barometers. The small honesty branches are secured simply by pushing them into the twiggy wreath base, while the thistles are fastened on with short lengths of florist's wire. The garland is then finished off beautifully with a sumptuous grey-green satin ribbon at the top.

1 | Break the honesty branches up into smaller sprays and push them individually at an angle into the twiggy wreath base, working around the wreath to make sure the base is well covered. Leave a small space at the top in which to tie the ribbon. You will find that the honesty holds firm and needs no extra form of attachment.

2 | Shorten the stems of the silver thistles and make a hole through the top of the stems with the bradawl. Push a length of florist's wire through each stem and twist to hold securely.

3 | Space the thistles evenly around the wreath and secure by pushing the two ends of the wire through the honesty and around the back of the twiggy base. Twist from behind to hold the thistles securely.

4 | Tie the ribbon in a generous bow. Thread a piece of wire through the back of the knot and wire the bow onto the wreath in the same manner as the thistles. The extra wire behind can be twisted into a loop from which to hang the wreath.

Miniature Papier Mâché Houses

★

Thin card

★

Scissors

★

PVA glue

★

Fungicide-free wallpaper paste

★

Recycled white paper

★

Acrylic gesso

★

Paintbrush

★

Acrylic paint in blue, pink, orange and yellow

★

Selection of silver cord, braids and ric-rac

★

Selection of shaped sequins

★

Adhesive tape

These bright and colourful little houses were inspired by the old Polish custom of making Christmas cribs in the form of houses, churches and amazing palaces. They were made from card, wrapped in paper and highly decorated with glittery foils. Groups of carol singers carried the largest examples around the villages at Christmas. The tradition continues to this day and many towns hold competitions to judge the best crib.

1 Draw the elements of the house on to the card – base, back, front, two gable ends, two roof pieces and roof ridge – and cut out. Using PVA glue, stick the front and sides to the base and to each other. Hold in place for a minute or two until the glue begins to set, then add the front and back sections of the roof, finally adding the roof ridge. Allow the glue to dry.

2 Mix the wallpaper paste and tear the paper up into small squares. Smear lightly with the paste and cover the entire house with paper, taking it under the base. Allow to dry on a radiator or in a warm place for an hour.

3 Paint the house with two coats of acrylic gesso, allowing it to dry thoroughly between each coat.

4 | Mix the blue acrylic paint on a saucer and paint each gable end – you may need to apply two coats for even coverage.

5 | Paint the front and back pink, the base and roof orange and the roof ridge yellow. Always clean the brush thoroughly between each different colour.

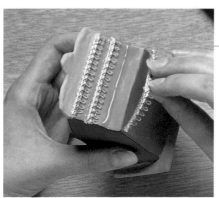

6 | Put three strips of the adhesive tape along the front of the roof and stick some of the decorative braid in place. Repeat on the back of the roof.

7 | Add the silver ric-rac to the front and back and stick the cord around all the edges of the base, house and roof. Dissect the blue gable ends with a cord.

8 | Lastly, add the sequin decoration, large blue stars at the front and back and smaller sequins along the roof ridge. Cut the leaves in half and arrange on either side of the silver cord on the gable ends and finish off with two pink flowers.

Citrus Pomanders

Traditional citrus pomanders simply decorated with cloves have been made since the sixteenth century. They were thought to have been carried to ward off disease.

The unusual and inventive variations of Elizabethan pomanders opposite are made by sticking cloves into the orange in spirals, diamonds and stars. You can then roll them in the ancient recipe of powdered orrisroot and sweet spices to preserve them. This should be done several weeks before Christmas for the best effect. The smaller pomanders are divided into segments with rows of cloves; each segment has been slit with a knife and they have been dried in a cool oven over many days.

1 | Draw the pattern clearly onto the skin of the orange with the black felt pen – simple designs are the best and most effective.

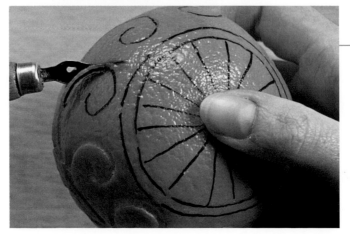

2 | Following the lines, carefully cut out the pattern with the lino cutting tool, keeping the blade of the tool moving away from you.

Clove-spiked Pomanders

1 Divide the orange into eight segments with lines of tightly packed cloves. The cloves will push through the peel quite easily.

2 Make long slits in the orange between the lines of cloves. Dry the pomanders in a very cool oven, preferably with the door open, for several days. The coolest oven of an Aga is ideal. A warm airing cupboard is a good alternative.

Glitzy Paper Chains

Rough paper

Gold paper

Gold spray paint

Ruler

Pencil

Scissors

★

Sequins

★

All-purpose adhesive

One of the most popular of children's decorations at Christmas, here is a glitzy version to add some glamour to this old favourite.

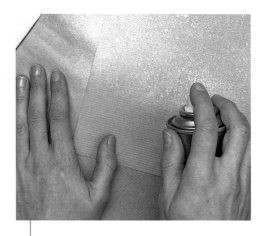

1 | Protect your worksurface with rough paper. Spray the back of your gold paper with gold paint so that the insides of the paper chains will glimmer just like the outsides once they are hanging on the tree.

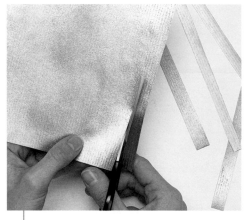

2 | Mark faint guidelines approximately 1cm (½in) apart on the paper with a ruler and pencil and then cut the paper into strips.

3 | On the outside of each strip, stick a sequin in the middle and at one end for some added sparkle.

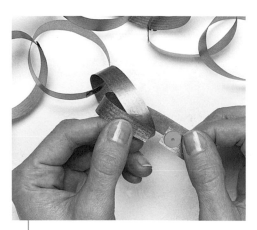

4 | Link the strips together, gluing the ends, to make one very long chain or several shorter ones to drape all over the tree.

Cinnamon Bundles

Simple to make, these bundles are especially effective when hung all over the tree and will create a lovely scent in your home.

1 Cut the pieces of cinnamon into lengths of about 5cm (2in).

2 Group the cut sticks into fours and tie together using a few pieces of raffia.

3 Tie the raffia ends together close to the bundle to secure and then again further away from the cinnamon sticks to form a hanging loop.

4 Rub the part of the raffia that is tied around each cinnamon bundle with the gilt cream.

Snowflakes

These glittery snowflakes look wonderful strung together or placed individually on the tree lights or above your mantlepiece.

YOU WILL NEED

★

Silver tissue paper

★

Pencil

★

Scissors

★

Rubber-based adhesive

★

Gold and silver glitters

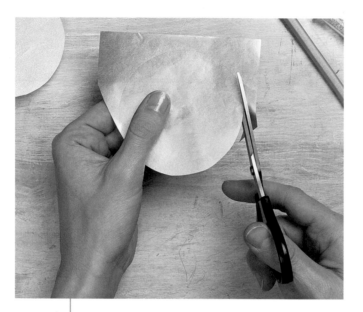

1 | Cut out small circles of silver tissue paper. These can be all the same size or varying, depending on the effect you desire.

2 | Fold each circle into eight by folding in half, in half again and then in half one more time.

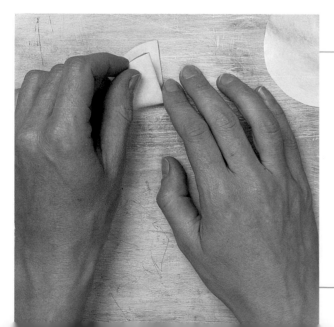

3 | Snip a pattern into each piece of tissue (remember that every snowflake is different). Make the pattern as intricate as you like but don't cut folds away completely or the flake will fall to pieces.

4 Embellish with glitter stuck on to adhesive. Do this on scrap paper to catch the glitter for recyling. If using the flakes on the lights, switch off and push the flakes well down the outsides of the plastic casings.

Tin Stars

This is the perfect project for young fingers as tracing and using glitter are always very popular crafts with kids.

1 | Trace the template on page 149 onto a piece of wax paper. Stick the tracing onto the foil paper using clear adhesive tape and draw over the design with the ballpoint pen. Press hard.

3 | Using a tin star as a template, draw around the star onto pieces of white card, allowing a 5mm (¼in) margin around the tin. Spread glue all over the card backings and stick the tin stars in the centre.

2 | Carefully cut out each star with the scissors (not your best pair as they will be blunted).

4 | Sprinkle the card surround with glitter. If you do this over a piece of paper it will be easier to tip excess glitter back into the tube to be used again. Dust off excess glitter and thread with fishing line for a loop.

Tin Angel

YOU WILL NEED

★

Templates (see pages 149–150)

★

Pencil

★

Wax paper

★

Scissors

★

Foil paper

★

Clear adhesive tape

★

Dry ballpoint pen

★

Florist's foam

★

Kitchen knife

★

Gold card

★

Rubber-based adhesive

★

*Short length of Christmas
tree candle*

★

String of silver sequins

Don't be deterred by the length of this project. Although care needs to be taken, the end result is worth it. The little angel can either perch by the hearth or stand at the foot of the tree.

1 Trace the wings, sleeves, crown and skirt templates onto wax paper and roughly cut out the shapes. Stick onto foil paper and draw firmly over the outlines and details with the dry ballpoint pen.

2 Cut the angel's body from a piece of florist's foam. The finished piece looks like a pyramid with the top sliced off and the base measures 3 x 2cm (1½ x 1in).

3 Cut out a small rectangular piece of foil paper and make a hole in the centre. Then use the foil to cover the top of the florist's foam body.

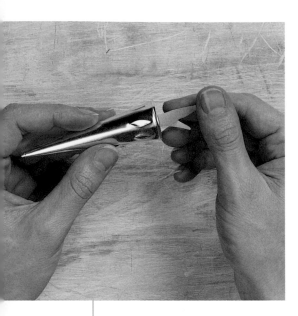

6 To make the angel's hair, cut out a small rectangular piece of foil and snip along one edge. Stick the hair around the candle with the face on it, ensuring that the fringe is at the front.

4 Cut out the prepared sleeves from the foil, roll into cones and fasten on the inside with adhesive tape. Cut the hands from the gold paper and stick with adhesive into the wide end of the sleeves.

7 Cut out the prepared crown from the foil paper and stick over the hair with the rubber-based adhesive.

5 Draw the face onto a small oval-shaped piece of gold paper and stick onto the candle. Pare the candle down slightly with a sharp knife if the one you have is too large.

8 Cut out the prepared skirt, roll into a cone and fasten on the inside with adhesive tape. Then stick the body and the skirt together using the rubber-based adhesive.

9 For the top part of the angel's dress, wind a string of silver sequins around the body. Start from the waist and work upwards, gluing the sequins into place at the top.

11 Add the head, pushing the bottom of the candle (covered with glue) firmly into the hole made in the foil and through into the florist's foam.

10 Flatten the top of the sleeve cones and fold over 5mm (¼in) to make a hinge. Slot the hinges into the top of the body between the sequins and florist's foam.

12 Cut out the prepared wings from the foil paper and stick them to the back of the angel with the rubber-based adhesive. The top of the wings should be aligned about half way up her head.

Gilded Pot

This very clever technique will transform an old pot into a beautiful container. Parts of the pot showing through will give it a more aged look.

1 Paint the pot with acrylic size. Paint well over the rim of the pot as this area will be very prominent. Leave the size to dry for a few minutes until it is clear.

3 Gently peel the backing off the transfer leaf. Don't worry if some of the terracotta shows through.

2 Press on sheets of gold transfer leaf using the stiff paintbrush.

4 Brush off any excess bits with the same dry paintbrush.

Holly Sprigs

Here is an incredibly quick and easy project that combines fresh holly leaves with fake berries.

1 | Paint some of the leaves of a sprig of holly with liquid leaf, applying it with the paintbrush.

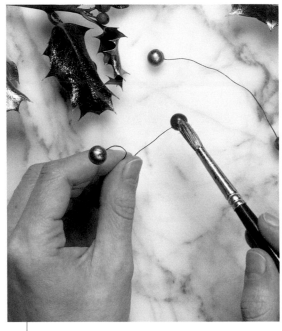

3 | Paint some of the fake holly berries with the liquid leaf.

2 | Paint the remaining leaves using blobs of glitter from the glitter pen.

4 | To complete each sprig, wire the fake berries onto the painted leaves.

Golden Star

YOU WILL NEED

★

Scissors

★

Gold paper

★

Clear adhesive tape

★

All-purpose adhesive

★

Stiff white card

★

Gold cord

★

1 gold sequin

Some very simple folds on gold paper and, hey presto, a golden star to place above your threshold or in a doorway is created.

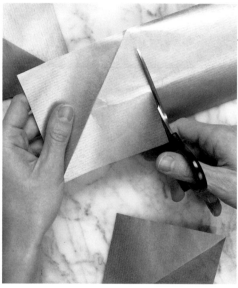

1 | Cut out five 10cm (4in) squares of gold paper. Fold each square in half diagonally and open out flat again.

2 | On the reverse side, bring one corner to meet the centre fold. Press flat, repeat on the other side and open out. Using the folds, make a 3-D shape, overlapping the outside edges and securing with tape.

3 | Repeat with each square of gold paper. Stick the bottom of each point onto a piece of stiff card, butting them up close and placing a piece of adhesive tape under the centre points of the stars.

4 Cut out the star, trimming as close as possible to the gold paper

Holly and Ivy Garland

YOU WILL NEED

★

4 garland cylinders

★

Sharp knife

★

Florist's foam

★

Holly and ivy branches

★

Newspaper

★

Adhesive tape

★

Ribbon

★

Florist's wire

Greenery, picked fresh from the garden, can be made into a Christmas decoration in moments. To make this lush green design you will need four garland cylinders bought from a florist's shop.

1   Using a sharp knife, cut a block of florist's foam to fit each cylinder, then clip and hook the cylinders together to link them up.

2   Cut branches of holly and ivy to the lengths you require. Trim them, leaving at least a 4cm (1⅛in) stalk with a sharply cut end to spear into the florist's foam.

3   Fill out the shape of the garland with the holly and ivy, leaving several trails of ivy dangling as if it were growing naturally. Try to give the whole garland the informal arrangement of its natural environment.

4 | To make the miniature crackers, cut 5cm (2in) width strips from folded newspaper. Roll each one into a compact 'sausage', fastened with clear adhesive tape, to form the central core. Cut a selection of wrapping papers into 12cm (5in) pieces.

5 | Pinch together the ends of paper around the central roll to form the cracker shape and secure by looping a narrow ribbon round twice. Tie the ribbons in a bow and cut off the surplus paper at the ends of the crackers to neaten them.

6 | Thread florist's wire behind the ribbon bows and then twist tightly to form a spear. Push this straight into the florist's foam base to secure the crackers among the leaves of the garland.

Tinsel Card Garland

YOU WILL NEED

Template (see page 150)

Shiny red card

Florist's wire

Silver paper clips

Silver tinsel

Double-sided tape

Red ribbon

This star-shaped decoration provides another interesting way to hang your Christmas cards. Make three firm circles, 31cm (12in) in diameter, from florist's wire and bind them with masking tape.

1 | Cut three stars out of shiny red card. Position a star in the centre of one of the circles and mark the spots where the five points meet the circle.

2 | Using florist's wire, attach five silver paper clips to the marked positions, then add another clip in each of the spaces between. Wind lengths of tinsel around the rings, making sure that none of the tape is visible. Secure the ends of the tinsel in one of the paper clips.

3 | Attach double-sided tape to the back of the points of each star and stick them onto the ring to align with the five paper clips. Bind pairs of holly leaves together with florist's wire and stick a narrow bow of red ribbon to them with double-sided tape. Wire the holly onto the ring, between the star points, at the base of a paper clip.

4 | To assemble the garland, place the rings side by side and tie a red ribbon, leaving long ends, around adjoining paper clips on two circles (the joins will be covered by a card). Tie ribbon around the end rings; use the long lengths of ribbon for hanging the garland up. Arrange your cards, using the extended paper clips to hold them in position. Stick a card in the centre of each star shape using double-sided tape.

YOU WILL NEED

Glass candle lantern

Plain paper

Scissors

Spray glue

Turquoise, royal blue, purple, gold, purple and clear water-based glass paints

Paper plate

Sponges

Craft knife

Glass stars

Silicone glue

Star-Burst Candle Lantern

This project is easy to make and stunning to look at. The most time-consuming part is cutting out all the paper masks, so if you have children get them to help. Once this is done, the lantern is quick to make.

1 | Photocopy a design as many times as you need and cut out the paper masks. Use spray glue to stick the paper to the glass.

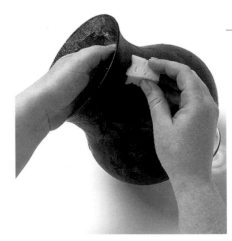

3 | Sponge royal blue paint around the base of the lantern. This will blend with the turquoise paint to give a graduated colour effect.

2 | Sponge on your first colour. Start with the lightest colours first, in this case, turquoise. Do not sponge right up to the rim of the lantern. Work quickly so that the paint doesn't dry before you add the next colour, or the colours won't blend well.

4 | Using a clean piece of sponge, apply purple paint to the rim of the lantern, overlapping the turquoise paint a little.

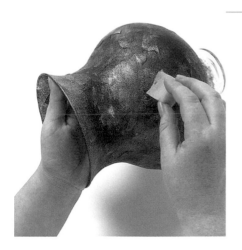

5 Using another clean sponge, apply a little gold paint around each of the paper masks and around the base and rim of the lantern.

8 As a finishing touch, use silicone glue to stick a glass star to the centre of each design.

6 Use the tip of a craft knife and then your fingers to peel off the paper masks.

7 Finally, using a clean sponge, sponge some clear paint over the clear designs. This will make them look less stark and give a twinkle to the glass when the candlelight shines through them.

Beaded Rainbow Catcher

YOU WILL NEED

Template (see page 151)

Sheet of extra thick film

Gold outliner

Hot stencil cutter

Clear water-based glass paint

Fine paintbrush

Clear, pale pink, bright pink, gold, purple and blue beads

Silicone glue

Round crystal to fit the hole in the design

Nylon thread

Hang this rainbow catcher in a window and when the sun shines through the crystal in the centre, rainbows will appear all over the walls of the room. It is best to make these catchers from rigid, extra thick, plastic film, as glass would be very difficult to cut to shape. Choose translucent and iridescent beads that will catch the sunlight.

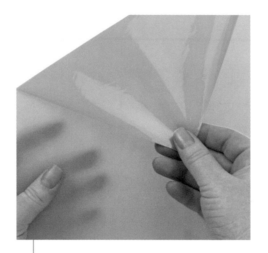

1 The extra thick film comes with a protective backing sheet. Peel this off at least one hour before you outline onto it. If you don't do this, the static electricity will make your outliner jump all over the place.

2 Place your design (there are two variation template designs on page 151) under the film and outline it in gold. Leave it to dry and then cut the shape out with sturdy scissors.

3 Use a hot stencil cutter to cut out the circle in the middle of the design. It is a good idea at this time to check that the crystal fits the hole; it should sit in it without falling right through.

4 Starting in the middle, brush clear paint into a few sections of the design. Try not to get paint on the gold outliner or the beads will stick to it and the gold won't show.

5 | Drop clear beads onto the paint. If you fold a strip of paper in half and decant a small amount of beads into this it makes it easier to drop them in the right spot. When you have beaded a few sections, paint a few more and then bead them. Work right around the design in this way.

6 | When all beads are in position, drop some clear paint over them to help hold them in place. Leave to dry for a short while.

7 Add the pale pink beads in the same way. Use the tip of your paintbrush to nudge any stray beads into the right place. Next, add the bright pink beads and leave them to dry. A hair dryer can be used to speed up the drying time, but don't hold it too close, as you don't want to blow the beads away.

9 Place the beaded film over a cup and place the crystal in the hole. Squeeze some silicone glue into an outlining bag and pipe it around the base of the crystal, so that the glue touches the crystal and the film. Leave to dry. When the glue is dry, turn the rainbow catcher over and silicone the back of the crystal in the same way. Leave to dry.

8 Next add the gold beads, followed by the purple beads. Finally, add the blue beads. Leave to dry completely.

10 Then, with a bradawl or hot stencil cutter, make a small hole at the top of the rainbow catcher. Push some nylon thread through the hole to hang the rainbow catcher from.

Granules and Moulds

Plastic granules work brilliantly in moulds. Choose moulds that are simple, strong shapes – you won't get good results from detailed moulds as the granules won't go into all the nooks and crannies. You can get lots of moulds for free. Next time you unpack your shopping, just see how many products come in plastic shapes. Even yogurt pots and tubs can be used (save the lids to make stencils from).

1 Grease the mould with margarine, painting it on with a paintbrush. Make sure you cover the whole surface as if any of the granules stick, the shape will be damaged. Remember that a mould only makes half a shape, so for a whole one you need two moulds. Here we are making a sphere.

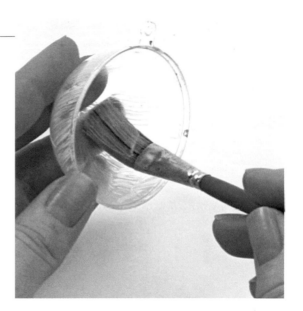

2 Follow the technique used to mix the granules for the biscuit cutters, then spoon them into the mould.

3 To make a hollow sphere, use the back of a spoon to ease the layer of granules up the sides of the moulds. Make the top edges as flat as possible. Leave to dry overnight.

4 Tap the half-sphere out of the mould. If it sticks, just dip it into warm water for a few seconds and it will drop out. Wash off any grease and dry the half-sphere.

6 To turn the sphere into a hanging bauble, first knot the ends of a length of ribbon together.

5 If the edges are a bit rough, place the half-sphere edge-down onto some coarse sandpaper and sand them smoother.

7 Squeeze some craft or silicone glue around the edge of one half-sphere. Place the ribbon so that the knot is on the inside of the half-sphere.

8 Press the two half-spheres together to make a whole sphere. Put a strip of masking tape around the sphere to hold it together while the glue dries.

10 Wind the ribbon around the sphere, covering the join and glue the other end down. You may find that you need another blob of glue at the bottom of the sphere to hold the ribbon in place. Glue the other length around the sphere at right angles to the first length.

9 For a neat finish, cut two lengths of ribbon to the same size as the circumference of the sphere. Squeeze a blob of silicone glue onto the sphere on the join, next to the hanging ribbon.

11 Make tiny gold spots all over the bauble by squeezing on dots of outliner straight from the bottle.

Decorating *the* Tree

Golden Swag

YOU WILL NEED

▲

Metallic organdie

▲

Gold metallic ribbon –
9 lengths of 35cm (14in) long by
3.5cm (1¼in) wide

▲

Dried flowerheads

▲

Gold spray

▲

2 gold tassels

▲

Needle

▲

Matching thread

▲

Pins

This sumptuous golden swag has the rare and precious feel of an antique fabric. It has been cleverly cut on the bias from exquisite organdie which is loosely woven with silk and metallic threads to produce a stunning, semi-transparent material. Here it has been appliquéd with pale golden ribbons and subtle, gold-sprayed dried flowerheads to enhance your tree at Christmas.

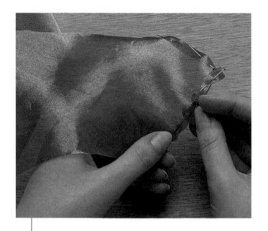

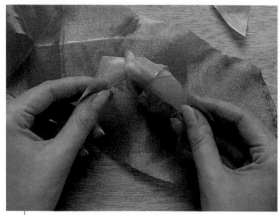

1 | Cut a length of organdie on the bias (2.3m (90in) long by 12.5cm (5in) wide. Cut both ends into a point, turn over a small hem and pin to hold in place. Hand stitch neatly with running stitch and remove the pins.

2 | Lay a length of gold metallic ribbon across the fabric 10cm (4in) from the end, pin in the middle and stitch firmly in place across the width of the ribbon. Tie the ribbon loosely into a double knot and neaten the ends.

3 | Spray the dried flowerheads very lightly with the gold spray to give just a hint of gold. Allow to dry. Lay a flowerhead onto the background 10cm (4in) from the ribbon and stitch in place around the stem.

4 Continue adding ribbons and flowerheads alternately in this manner along the whole length of the swag. Finally, sew the gold tassels in place on each of the pointed ends.

Glittery Net Hearts

YOU WILL NEED

▲

Template (see page 152)

▲

Scissors

▲

Scraps of coloured net

▲

Collection of glittery candy wrappers

▲

Pink, red and silver sequins

▲

Pins

▲

Needle

▲

Invisible thread

These original and adaptable little tree decorations are so simple and inexpensive to make from scraps of coloured net, sequins and saved candy wrappers. Light and flexible, they can be easily tucked into the branches of your Christmas tree.

The principle of sewing objects in-between two transparent layers could be applied in many different ways – tiny shells between sheets of iridescent cellophane, or miniature jewels enclosed in metallic organdie.

3 Carefully insert six little squares between the two layers of net, pinning through the net (not the paper) to hold each one in place. The sequins are positioned in the same way.

1 Draw a heart on the card and cut out the template. Pin the heart template onto a double thickness of net and neatly cut around.

2 Cut the glittery candy wrappers into small squares, selecting colours of a similar tonal range.

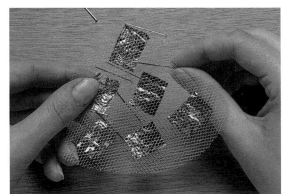

4 Using the invisible thread, sew around each square or sequin, carefully enclosing it between the two net layers. Remove the pins as you sew.

Braided Baubles

YOU WILL NEED

▲

Coloured tissue paper

▲

Polystyrene balls

▲

Rubber-based adhesive

▲

Gold cord

▲

Dressmaker's pins

▲

Fancy braid

▲

Sequins

▲

Coloured pins

Braids, ribbons and sequins are held in place quickly and simply with dressmaker's pins, making this project very versatile. You can create quirky or more traditional baubles, depending on your design.

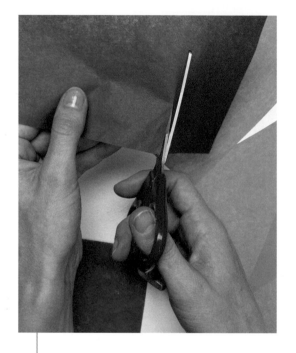

1 | Cut out strips of tissue paper that are long and wide enough to wrap around the polystyrene balls.

2 | Wrap the tissue paper around the balls and glue into place at the top and bottom with the rubber-based adhesive.

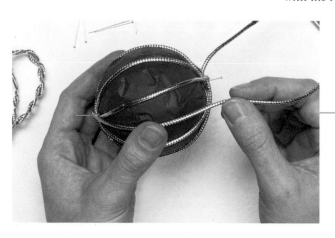

3 | Wind the gold cord around each ball to make whatever pattern you want. Use the dressmaker's pins to invisibly secure it, gluing the pins in place to prevent them falling out.

4 | Embellish further using fancy braid. Here the braid overlaps alternate strands of the cord, but there are many other ways in which you can use it.

Fabric Star

The brighter the fabric the better. Any colourful material will do, but the two-way colours of silk dupion add style to these tactile and beautifully padded star decorations.

YOU WILL NEED

▲

Template (see page 152)

▲

Stiff card

▲

Scissors

▲

Fabric pencil or chalk

▲

Selection of coloured silk dupion

▲

Needle

▲

Thread

▲

Wadding (batting)

▲

Beads, sequins and braids

▲

Small glass beads

1 Transfer the template onto a piece of stiff card and cut out. Draw around it onto the pieces of fabric (two for each star) using the fabric pencil or chalk. Then cut out the stars.

2 Join together two stars of different colours with right sides facing. Stitch together by hand or with a machine, leaving a small gap for turning through. Turn right sides out and then stuff with wadding (batting).

3 If necessary, poke out the corners with a small pair of scissors as you stuff. Turn in the final opening and sew it up by hand with tiny overstitches.

4 Embellish the stars with beads, sequins and braids. For a final twinkle, sew small glass beads onto each point and then hang the stars on the tree.

Felt Birds

YOU WILL NEED

▲

Templates (see page 153)

▲

Coloured felt

▲

Scissors

▲

Rubber-based adhesive

▲

Paintbrush

▲

Needle

▲

Coloured embroidery threads

▲

Wadding (batting)

▲

Blue glass beads

The beauty of felt is that there are no fraying edges to contend with. Cut out your shapes and they will remain the same throughout all your Christmases to come.

1 Cut out a square of felt, the colour that you would like the bird's body to be. Cut out the tail pieces and wings from other colours. Cut a small triangle of yellow felt for the beak.

3 Fold the square over into a triangle and, starting from the end with the beak, sew the two edges together using herringbone stitch in a contrasting coloured embroidery thread.

2 Stick the beak onto one corner of the body using the rubber-based adhesive.

4 When you have about 3cm (1¼in) left to stitch, stuff the bird with the wadding. Do not sew the opening closed.

5 | Roll two different coloured tail pieces together. Push the straight end of the tail piece into the body through the hole where the wadding was stuffed and stitch in place to secure.

6 | Attach the wings using a contrasting coloured thread and then embellish the middle of the wing with an embroidered sunburst shape. Sew on small glass beads as eyes and attach a loop of thread to the bird's back for hanging it from the tree.

Felt Star

YOU WILL NEED

▲

Template (see page 152)

▲

Green and red felt

▲

Wadding (batting)

▲

Needle

▲

*Red and green embroidery
threads*

▲

Red, gold and green beads

The embroidery stitches used for this project are straightforward, making the star ideal for a child to make. Coloured beads sewn over the edges add a touch of quirkiness to these stars.

1 │ Use red for the front and green for the back and the small star on the front.

2 │ Sew the small green star onto the front of the red one using small overstitches and red embroidery thread. Then embellish it with red and gold beads (see the picture opposite for a suggested design).

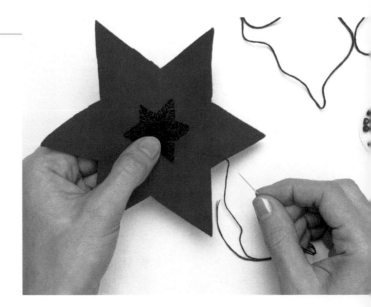

3 Sew a 1cm (½in) wide strip of felt onto the large green star, attaching it at both ends with neat overstitches to form a loop by which to attach the star to the top of the tree.

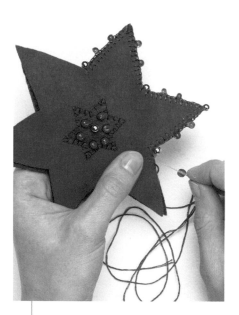

4 Sew the two sides of the star together using blanket stitch and lightly pad it with wadding (batting) as you go. Thread a bead onto the thread every third stitch or so, alternating the colours in a regular pattern.

Icicles

YOU WILL NEED

▲

Template (see page 153)

▲

Pencil

▲

Wax paper

▲

Scissors

▲

Foil paper

▲

Clear adhesive tape

▲

Ballpoint pen

▲

Glass beads

▲

Fishing line

▲

Rubber-based adhesive

The foil paper that is used for this project and for others in the book is special foil available from artists' suppliers. If you have a garden, these lovely decorations can hang from the branches of a tree.

1 | Trace the templates onto a piece of wax paper and roughly cut around the outlines.

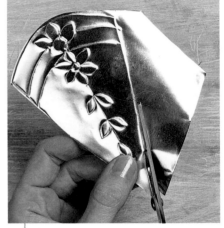

3 | Cut out the shapes from the foil paper but don't use your best scissors!

2 | Stick the tracing onto the foil paper using clear adhesive tape and draw over the detailed patterns using the ballpoint pen. Press hard.

4 | Roll each of the parts into a cone shape and carefully stick them together on the inside using small pieces of clear adhesive tape.

5 | Take a piece of fishing line, tie a knot at one end and then thread some glass beads onto it. Thread the other end of the line through the point of the largest cone. Fasten on the inside using adhesive tape.

6 | Take a small piece of paper and screw it up into a ball. Then glue both parts of the icicle onto the paper so that the larger piece of foil overlaps the smaller.

Beaded Baubles

YOU WILL NEED

▲

Polystyrene balls in assorted sizes

▲

Foil paper

▲

Scissors

▲

Rubber-based adhesive

▲

Small cylindrical glass sleeves

▲

Small plain glass beads

▲

Silver sequins

▲

Dressmaker's pins

▲

All-purpose adhesive

▲

Fishing line

Dressmaker's pins are available in different lengths. For this project it is best to use the longest you can find so that you can use a variety of materials to decorate these highly versatile polystyrene balls.

1 Cut out rectangles of foil paper large enough to wrap around the polystyrene balls.

3 Dip the pointed end of the decorated pin into the adhesive. Then push it into the covered polystyrene ball as far as possible so that none of the uncovered pin shows.

2 Thread three cylindrical glass sleeves, a plain glass bead and a silver sequin onto a dressmaker's pin.

4 Repeat steps 2 and 3 until the whole ball is covered. Add some fishing line in a loop for hanging from the tree. Fasten the fishing line to the ball with a pin stuck in place as before.

Twinkle Twinkle

YOU WILL NEED

Scissors

▲

Coloured thread

▲

Hole punch

This simple star can be hung on the wall or from the ceiling, as well as on the Christmas tree. It is made up of equilateral triangles, which enable the star's points to fold in half to create a three-dimensional shape.

1 | Trace and cut out a star template that is made up of equilateral triangles (each star point should be at 60°).

2 | Fold the star in half three times between opposite points. Next fold it in half three times between opposite angles as shown. Every angle and point should now have a fold in it.

3 | The star will now easily bend into its sculptured shape. Make a small hole in its top point with a hole punch or a skewer, then put some thread through the hole to hang it up.

Little Boxes

YOU WILL NEED

▲

Scissors

▲

All-purpose adhesive

▲

Wrapping paper

▲

Ribbons

These little boxes make charming tree decorations. If you haven't got any suitable ones that you can wrap for the tree, you can easily make your own from card, cut from a simple 'Latin cross' template.

1 | For a cube, you need to mark out a Latin cross shape. The lower arm of the cross should be twice as long as the top and side arms. Also add a 1.5cm (½in) border to all arms except the top one for gluing the cube together.

2 | Fold along all the lines as shown, then bring the cube together, gluing all the sides in place.

3 | Now simply wrap the box in attractive paper and tie it with ribbons and bows to look like a parcel. Pop it on or under the tree.

Satin Presents

These pretty ornaments can be made any size. For a cube shape the pattern is a Latin cross (as shown), the long piece being twice the length of the others; all the other sides must be of equal length.

YOU WILL NEED

Satin

▲

Iron-on interfacing

▲

Thread

▲

Needle

▲

Polyester filling

▲

Ribbons and bows

1 | Cut this shape out in satin, then cut a piece of iron-on interfacing, 1cm (½in) smaller all round. Iron on the interfacing. Also iron in creases to form the sides of the cube.

2 | Placing right sides together, sew all the seams, using a small running stitch, cutting into the corners and using the interfacing edge as a seamline.

3 | Leave one edge open so that you can turn the cube right side out. Stuff it with polyester filling, then slipstitch the opening edges together. Decorate the cube with ribbon and bows, then set it on a branch of your Christmas tree. For a rectangular box, simply widen the long section of the cross. The round box is a purchased box with satin glued onto it.

Santa Faces

These jolly Santa faces will add Christmas cheer to the tree. They make an ideal project for children as the techniques are simple.

1 | Design a santa face and cut out all the pieces of felt, using your template. Glue the main face piece to a piece of card. When it is dry, cut around it.

2 | All you have to do now is glue on all the other pieces. The nose and cheeks are affixed before the moustache, which goes on top.

3 | Place a loop of thread under the circle on the top of the hat, to hang up the face. Glue on two dark sequins to represent the eyes.

Mini Trees

YOU WILL NEED

▲

Scissors

▲

Coloured felt

▲

Thread

▲

Needle

▲

Wadding (batting)

▲

Sequins

▲

*Tinsel and gold or silver
thread*

Another fun tree decoration that will last from year to year. You can create your own tree shapes or trace a design from a Christmas card.

1 | Cut the tree shapes out in two different colours of felt, cutting two each of tree and pot. Place the two tree shapes together and work buttonhole stitch around the edges, leaving the trunk end open.

2 | Stuff the tree lightly with a little filling. Now buttonhole stitch around the pot, leaving the top open. Slip the trunk into the pot and then lightly stuff the pot. Sew the tree and pot together at the sides.

3 | Sew a little bow to the top of the pot and decorate the tree with sequins and tinsel. Fix some gold or silver thread under the star on the top of the tree, so you can hang it up.

Little Crackers

YOU WILL NEED
▲

Thin card or cartridge paper

▲

Adhesive tape

▲

Coloured crepe or foil paper

▲

Ribbon

▲

Double-sided adhesive tape

These colourful crackers can be hung on the Christmas tree or on the wall. For a surprise, add a little gift or secret note and insert before you seal the ends.

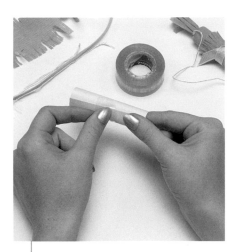

1 First take a piece of cartridge (drawing) paper or light card about 8cm (3in) wide and long enough to roll into a tube. Hold it together with a little adhesive tape.

3 To decorate, cut some extra, narrow pieces of crepe or foil paper, fringe them at the edges and wrap them around the tube as before. Alternatively, tie a bow round the cracker or stick a silver star in the middle.

2 Cut a piece of crepe paper or foil twice as long as the tube and roll the tube in it. Stick the edges together with double-sided tape. Squeeze the paper together at both ends and tie some thread around them. Fluff out the ends and make small cuts in them to make a fringe.

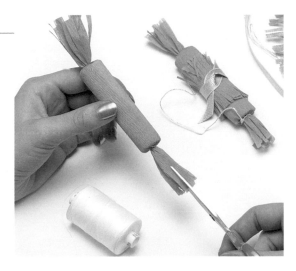

YOU WILL NEED

▲

Coloured felt

▲

Strip of imitation fur

▲

Thread

▲

Needle

▲

Sequins and bows

Stocking Fillers

These cute little boots can be used as tree decorations and would also look lovely hanging in front of the hearth.

1 Make a pattern for a Christmas stocking and cut it out double in one piece by placing the pattern on the fold of the felt. Cut a strip of fake fur to fit the stocking, about 5cm (2in) deep. Attach the fur to the felt, top and bottom, by hand, with small stitches.

2 Now overcast the two sides of the stocking together, starting at the ankle and working around the foot and up the front. Turn the stocking right side out.

3 Turn the fur down about 2.5cm (1in) to the right side, catching it down around the edge. Decorate the stocking with sequins, bows, etc. and sew a loop of ribbon just inside the edge to hang it.

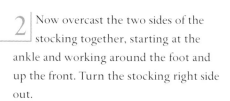

Ping Pong Puddings

▲

Table tennis balls

▲

Fine knitting needle

▲

Paintbrush

▲

Brown paint and varnish

▲

Modelling clay

▲

Thread

▲

Needle

▲

Scissors

▲

Red beads and foil holly leaves

Here is another cute tree decoration that is fun to make: tiny Christmas puddings. Table tennis balls are easy to decorate and the perfect shape and size for the tree.

1 You start with ordinary table tennis balls. Spear each one onto a fine knitting needle and paint it brown. After two or three coats, for a dark rich colour, finish off with a clear varnish to give the 'puddings' a lovely shine.

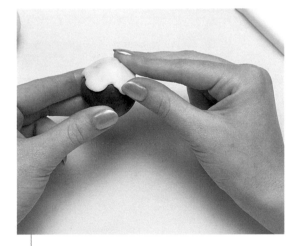

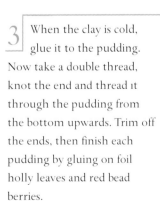

3 When the clay is cold, glue it to the pudding. Now take a double thread, knot the end and thread it through the pudding from the bottom upwards. Trim off the ends, then finish each pudding by gluing on foil holly leaves and red bead berries.

2 Now take some modelling clay, the sort you can bake in the oven and roll it into a ball, the same size as the table tennis balls. Over this, mould a thick circle of white clay, to look like custard sauce. Bake this in the oven and then remove it from the clay ball straight away and pop it onto a pudding.

Let's Pretend

YOU WILL NEED

▲

Lightweight card

▲

Pencil

▲

Coloured paint

▲

Thread or ribbon

▲

Tinsel wire

These three-dimensional baubles are simple for children to make and will give a funky retro look to your tree.

1 | First cut some circles, with a little loop on the top, from some lightweight card. Now mark out a pattern on each in pencil. Simple zigzags and curved lines are effective, but not too complicated to fill in.

2 | Paint each bauble with several different colours, waiting for each to dry before painting the next. If you have some gold or silver paint, make good use of this, as it is very effective. Use black to make definite lines between colours.

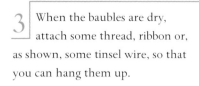

3 | When the baubles are dry, attach some thread, ribbon or, as shown, some tinsel wire, so that you can hang them up.

Fairy on the Tree

YOU WILL NEED

▲

Foil paper

▲

Scissors

▲

Adhesive tape

▲

Pink pipe cleaner

▲

Doily

▲

Double-sided tape

▲

*Table-tennis ball, toothpicks,
silver pen*

This traditional Christmas tree-top decoration makes a charming addition to the festivities. It can easily perch on the top of your tree without any need for a fixture.

1 Using a saucer, cut a circle out of silver foil paper. Cut the circle in half and fold one half into a cone, stapling it in place.

2 Take a pink pipe cleaner and tape it to the back of the cone; then bend it into arms and hands. On top of this fix a triangle of doily to represent wings, using double-sided tape. For the head, take an ordinary table tennis ball and skewer it onto a wooden toothpick (or cocktail stick). Push the stick into the cone.

3 The hair is made from grey crewel or Persian wool, stuck on with double-sided tape and the crown is a small piece of silver sequin waste. Draw the facial features with a fine-tipped silver pen. For the wand, spray a toothpick with silver paint and stick a small silver star on one end.

Cards, Tags *and* Giftwrap

Permanent black ink pad

Christmas tree stamp

Piece of metal foil

Embossing tool

Self-adhesive diamond dots

Double-sided tape

*White and dark green mulberry
paper*

Fine paintbrush

Water

Gold ink pad

Vellum

Gold embossing powder

Heat gun

Ruler

White blank card

Clear adhesive

Embossed Tree Card

Two different embossing techniques are used to make this textural Christmas greeting card. The gleaming foil is in high relief and the gold powder in low relief. You will need to buy a Christmas tree stamp and special embossing tool.

1 | Using the black ink pad, stamp the tree onto the metal foil. Remember to clean the stamp immediately. Leave the ink to dry completely. Working on the stamped side of the foil, draw over all the lines with the thin end of the embossing tool.

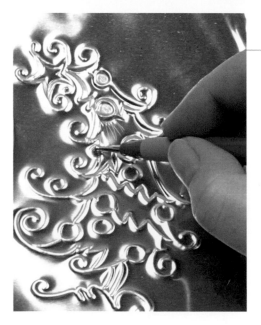

2 | Turn the foil over and, using the thick end of the tool, work into the inside sections of the tree. This pushes them the other way, so that they stand out on the right side. Start by working along the edges of the lines embossed in Step 1, then work across the sections. You can make embossed lines to suit the shape of design of the stamp you have used. Here, short vertical lines are used to represent the needles on the tree.

3 | Working on the stamped side, press the thin end of the tool into the foil around the tree to create a pattern of dots, giving a beaten metal look. You can work the dots in lines or swirls to complement the shape of the stamp.

4 | Stick a diamond dot onto each of the raised baubles on the tree.

5 | Using double-sided tape, stick the foil to the piece of white mulberry paper. Draw a line around the foil with a wet paintbrush and tear the paper. Pull out fibers to make a fringe. Repeat the process with the green mulberry paper to make a double mount.

6 Using the gold ink pad and embossing powder, emboss some trees onto vellum. Tear a strip of the embossed vellum approximately 3cm (1⅛in) wide. Spray the back with glue and stick it to the left-hand side of the card, close to the fold.

8 Tear a narrow strip off the front and back edges of the card.

7 Stick double-sided tape to the back of the foil panel. Peel off the paper backing and stick the panel to the card, just overlapping the edge of the vellum.

9 Dab clear adhesive onto the torn edges and sprinkle on gold embossing powder. Use a heat gun to melt the powder. The thicker the glue you use, the more textured the embossing will be since the glue bubbles when heated.

Snow Scene Card

YOU WILL NEED

21 x 30cm (8¼ x 12in) piece of watercolour paper

Broad paintbrush

Water

Prussian-blue artist's acrylic ink

Ruler

Snowflake rubber stamps

Clear embossing pad

White and silver sparkling embossing powder

Domestic iron

Fabric adhesive

22cm (8¾in) of white pom-pom braid

Decorated with embossed sparkly snowflakes against an inky-blue sky, this is a quick and easy seasonal card that needs few materials. When folded, the card fits a standard-size envelope.

1 | Using the broad paintbrush, apply water in a bold, undulating line across the paper, approximately a third of the way up. This will form the skyline, with the unpainted area below suggesting a snowy landscape. Brush water roughly across the upper two-thirds of the paper. For the best results, do not work right to the edges and do not over-wet the paper.

2 | Brush on the ink, allowing the colour to flood the wet area of the paper. Add more colour as required. The ink will gather in some areas, which will dry to a darker shade than others. The effect is random and will be different every time. Leave the paper to dry completely and, if necessary, place it under a few heavy books for a while to flatten it. Score and fold the paper to make a three-panel, concertina card.

3 | Consider the best positions for the embossed snowflakes and stamp the motifs onto the card using the rubber stamps and the embossing pad. Allow some of the motifs to cross onto the white area; the sparkling powder will ensure they show up.

4 | Sprinkle on the embossing powder and tip off the excess. Hold the card in front of the soleplate of a hot iron and let the powder melt and fuse together to complete the embossing process.

5 | Apply fabric adhesive to the flat part of the pom-pom braid. Stick it to the back of the left-hand panel. Leave to dry and then trim the ends level with the top and bottom of the card.

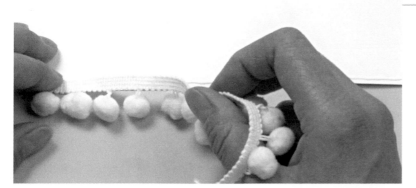

Snowy Christmas Tree Card

If every year you mean to make your own seasonal greetings cards, but never quite manage to find the time, then this is the project for you. You will spend longer writing and sealing them into envelopes than you did making the cards!

YOU WILL NEED

Cutting mat

Serrated knife

High density stencil sponge

White emulsion paint

Flat dish

*21 x 10cm (8¼ x 4in)
silver metallic single-fold card*

Glue pen

Small coloured cup sequins

All-purpose adhesive

Gold star sequin

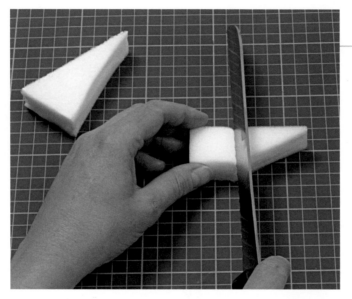

1 Working on a cutting mat, use a serrated knife to cut the sponge into an elongated triangle to make a simple Christmas tree shape 9cm (3½in) tall and 5cm (2in) across at the base. From the off cuts, cut a 2.5 x 2.5cm (1 x 1in) square, which will make the base and the trunk of the tree.

2 Decant some white paint into a flat dish and spread it out thinly. Dip the face of the triangular sponge into the paint, ensuring that the surface is evenly covered.

3 Press the triangle onto the front of the card, positioning it centrally and with the point approximately 4cm (1½in) down from the top. Gently lift the sponge off the card, being careful not to smudge the print.

4 Coat the face of the square sponge by dipping it into the white paint. Make the pot by stamping a square centrally, about 1cm (½in) below the tree. The trunk is made with the same square sponge held at an angle to make a narrow line, joining the tree to the pot. Leave to dry completely.

5 Use a glue pen to stick on a few sequin baubles and a dab of all-purpose adhesive to attach the star to the top of the tree.

Making Envelopes

The envelope you present a card in is important; your efforts will not be set off to best advantage by a tatty envelope! If you can't find a suitable ready-made envelope, have a non-standard size card, or if you want to use a particular paper to co-ordinate with a card, then making your own envelope is the best option. You should also consider decorating the envelope to match the card.

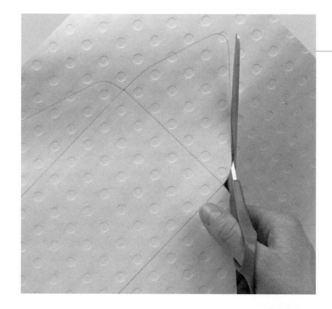

1 | Trace a template and transfer it onto the wrong side of the paper. Using scissors, cut out the envelope. If you are nervous about cutting straight lines, use a craft knife and steel ruler on a cutting mat to cut the long straight edges and cut out the curves with scissors.

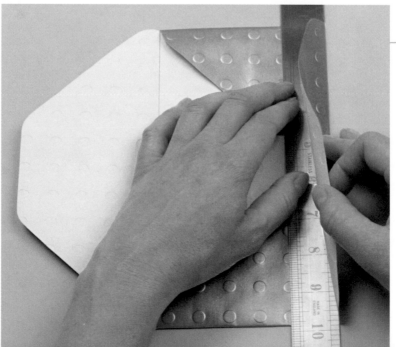

2 | With the paper right-side down, lay a steel ruler along one of the crease lines indicated on the template. Lift the flap up and fold it over the edge of the ruler to make a neat crease. Repeat on all four sides to make four flaps, then open the flaps out flat again.

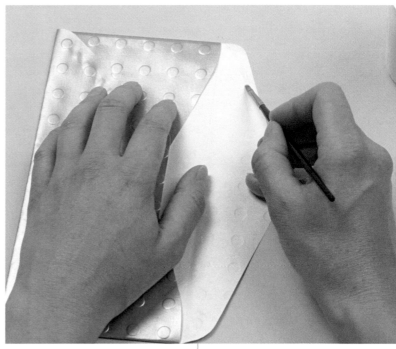

3 | Fold in the two side flaps only and apply a thin line of paper glue or special re-moistenable adhesive – along the edges that will be overlapped by the lower flap. Fold the lower flap up and press it down onto the glue. Leave to dry.

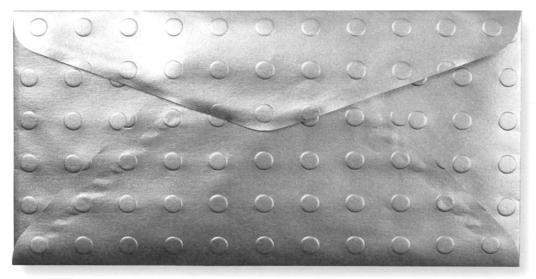

4 | The card can be sealed into the envelope in two ways. You can stick the top flap down with paper glue once the card is in the envelope, or you can use re-moistenable adhesive, as shown here. Paint a thin line of the adhesive along the inside edge of the top flap and leave it to dry. When you are ready to seal the card in the envelope, moisten the flap in the usual way to reactivate the adhesive, then stick the flap down.

Pillow Envelopes

YOU WILL NEED

*Tracing paper template
(see page 154)*

Card

Tracing wheel

Ruler

Scissors

Bone folder

Double-sided tape

A card with three-dimensional elements will be spoiled if it is squashed in a flat envelope. Such cards are best hand-delivered in a pillow envelope, which is easy to make from thin card. Enlarge or reduce the one you choose on a photocopier as required.

1 Trace the template and lay it on the right side of the card you want to make the envelope from. Run a dressmaker's tracing wheel over the template outline and crease lines to transfer them onto the card underneath. The indented lines will help you score the card and you do not have to make pencil marks that might be difficult to rub out. Use the wheel against a ruler along the straight edges and be careful not to make marks where they aren't needed, as you won't be able to remove them. Be especially careful around the indents, as the wheel can be tricky to maneuver around tight curves.

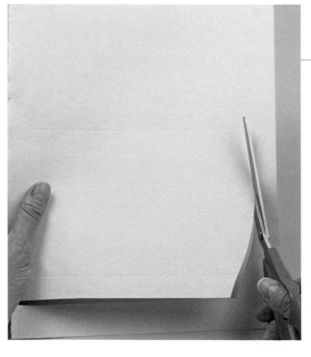

2 Remove the template and cut around the outer edges of the envelope with scissors, following the indented lines.

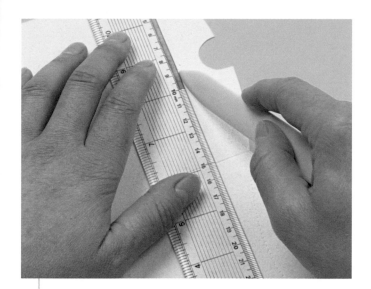

3 | Using a bone folder and ruler, score the curved and straight lines indicated by the remaining indented lines. The scoring will cover the indentations made by the tracing wheel, so it is important to be accurate. Along the curved lines, move the ruler around a bit at a time, so that it is always against the indentations and guiding the bone folder. To keep a scored line as smooth as possible, don't lift the bone folder off a line until you reach the end of it.

5 | Fold the extended flap in. Fold the taped edge over it and press it down to ensure that the tape sticks to the card right along its length.

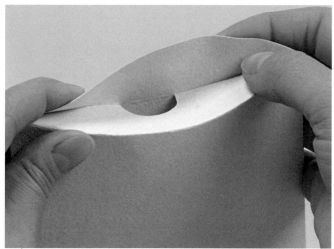

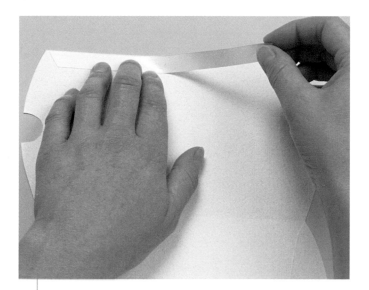

4 | Lay the envelope face down. Stick a strip of double-sided tape along the edge without the extended flap, trimming the tape at both ends where it meets the score lines so that it does not overlap them. The tape must not be wider than the extended flap or it will not be covered when the envelope is assembled. Peel the protective paper off the tape.

6 | Use your fingers and thumbs to gently press on either side of the curved scored lines to help coax the end sections over. The sections with the indents must be folded over first, so that the envelope can be opened easily.

Colourful Christmas Card

A modern interpretation of a favourite festive motif, this card can be worked in colours to suit your own Christmas theme. You could also try using the same techniques with other simple seasonal shapes, such as stars or snowflakes.

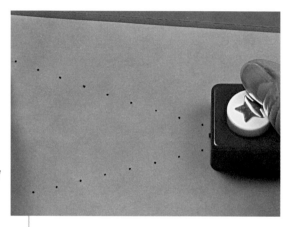

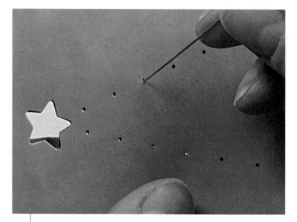

1 Trace the template onto the piece of tracing paper. Lay the paper over the card and punch out the star.

2 Using a pin, pierce holes through the card at the points marked on the template.

3 Thread the needle with a long length of embroidery thread and tie a knot in one end. Push the needle through the top left-hand hole, from back to front and pull the thread through right up to the knot.

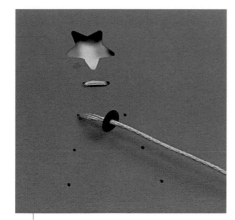

4 Take the needle down through the top right-hand hole to make the first stitch. Bring it back up through the next left-hand hole, thread on a sequin, then push the needle down through the parallel right-hand hole.

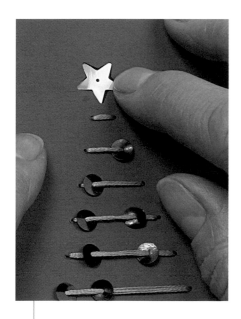

5 Continue, threading sequins onto each stitch, until the tree is complete. Fasten off the thread on the back. With the card closed, glue the star sequin through the star aperture to the inside back of the card.

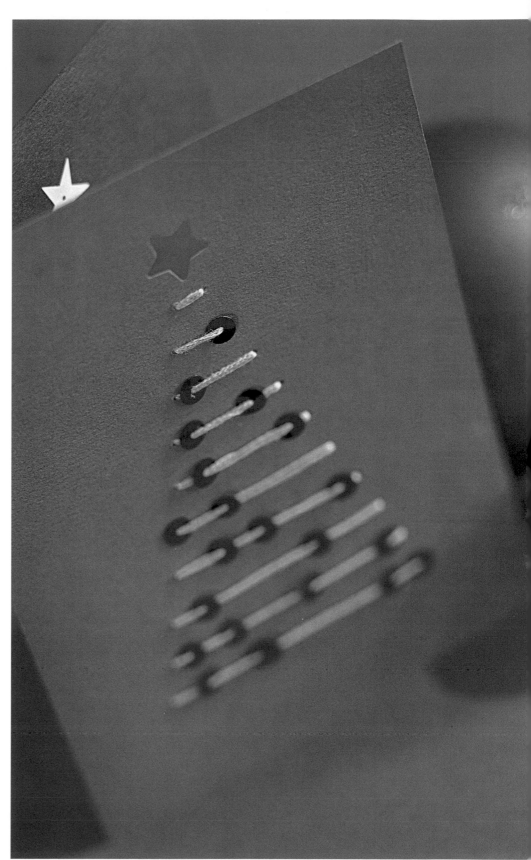

Shooting Stars Card

This dramatic card could be used for sending Christmas greetings or as an invite to a fireworks party. Invent cards for other occasions by changing the motif and colourway; heart-shaped sequins on a pink background for a valentine, perhaps.

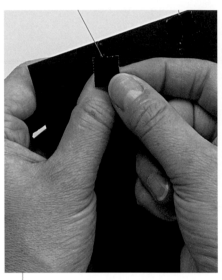

1 Score the card 8.5cm (3⅜in) from one short end. Machine curving lines from the score line across the short, front section of the card, using the main picture as a guide.

2 Fold the threads on the leading edge to the back and lay lengths of craft wire over them. Using black tape, tape the wire in place: on the front the wire should continue the lines of stitching.

3 Trim the wires so they are different lengths, both shorter than the back of the card. Put a dot of all-purpose adhesive on the back of a large star sequin and lay the end of a wire on it. Lay another sequin on top. Repeat the process with the end of the other wire.

4 Using the glue pen, put some tiny dots of adhesive on the front and the inside back of the card, positioning them around the lines of stitching and wires. Dampen the end of the cocktail stick, pick up tiny star sequins and put them on the dots of adhesive.

Christmas Gift Card

Spotted embossed wallpaper

Thick card

Paper glue

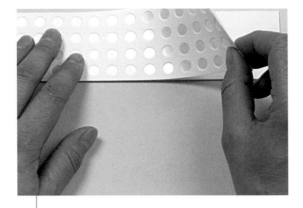

Craft knife

Steel ruler

Cutting mat

Narrow silver ribbon

Scissors

Double-sided tape

*12 x 17cm (4¾ x 6¾in)
smooth white card blank*

Sequins

Glue pen

Like all projects where large quantities are involved, it's best to set up a mini production line; preparing the squares, tying the ribbons, sticking the motifs to the cards and so on. Best of all, split the tasks between the family and have a jolly evening getting into the festive spirit.

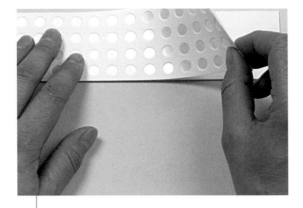

1 | Cut a 5cm (2⅛in) strip of wallpaper, taking the placing of the pattern into account. Using paper glue, stick the wallpaper to an identically sized piece of the thick card.

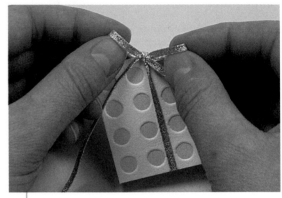

3 | Lay a length of ribbon around each square and tie the ends in a bow on one side. Trim the ends.

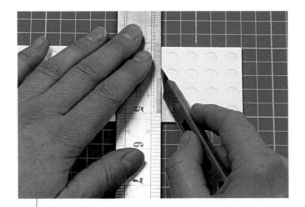

2 | Using the craft knife and steel ruler on the cutting mat, cut the strip into 5cm (2⅛in) squares.

4 | Working on the back, stick double-sided tape around the edges of the square. Peel off the backing and stick to the card blanks, as shown. Use the glue pen to stick sequins in some of the spots.

Christmas Tree Card

If you want to make your own Christmas cards but are put off by the quantity needed, this project is the solution. Do all the stamping first, followed by cutting and folding and finally all the detailing. Make the stamp to fit the cards.

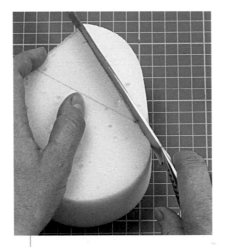

1 Using the felt-tip pen, draw a triangle on the bath sponge. Cut out the shape with the bread knife carefully to keep the edges straight and never cut toward your hand.

2 Spread some paint onto the plate. Using the paintbrush, brush green paint onto the surface of the sponge. Brush the paint on quite thickly.

3 Stamp the triangle onto the inside front of the card. The triangle must be centreed on the card front for the design to work. Leave to dry.

4 Lay the ruler down the middle of the tree. Score lines down the card from the top to the tip of the tree and from halfway across the base of the tree to the bottom of the card. (The line must be parallel to the leading edge of the card, so ensure that the top line touches the tip of the tree, but if the bottom line isn't exactly halfway across the base, it doesn't matter.)

5 | Using the craft knife on the cutting mat, cut from the scored line at the top of the tree, down the right-hand side and across the bottom to the scored line at the base of the tree. Cut just beyond the green edge so that the tree has a white border. If you are not confident about cutting freehand, use a steel rule to cut against.

6 | Fold the front of the card back on itself, folding it on the scored lines so that the tree comes to the front.

7 | Punch some small holes within the tree shape. Attach a star sequin to the top of the tree.

Star Pendant Card

This is a good presentation technique for pendants, Christmas decorations and other trinkets or mementos, as they can be removed and used by the recipient. For extra ornament, you could thread small beads onto the craft wire before you coil it.

1 Position the pendant on the card. Using a pin, pierce two holes in the front of the card, one through the hole in the pendant and the other just above the first one.

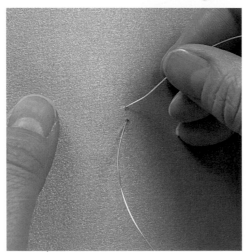

2 Cut approximately 50cm (20in) of craft wire. Working from the back of the card, poke one end of the wire through each hole.

3 Thread the pendant onto the lower piece of wire and push it right up to the card. Twist the wires tightly together.

4 Wind one end of the wire around a pencil to make a coil. Slide the wire coil off the pencil. Repeat the process with the other end.

5 Press the coils flat with your fingers.

Christmas Potpourri Boxes

This is a simple but elegant way to use empty gift boxes as containers for potpourri. We have selected a green and a black box. For the potpourri you can use your own selection of fragrant items or follow the 'recipe' in step 2.

YOU WILL NEED

Cow parsley

Gold spray paint

Empty gift boxes

Plastic wrap

1 | Take the lid off one of the boxes and lightly secure three whole flower heads of cow parsley diagonally across it. With aerosol spray paint, give the top of the box two light coats of gold paint.

2 | When the paint is dry, remove the parsley to reveal the unsprayed part of the box. This shows up as a pretty pattern through the paint. Now fix the gold-sprayed cow parsley to the other box lid and repeat the process. These boxes are filled with a festive mixture of small cones, tree bark and citrus peel. Cover the potpourri with plastic wrap before replacing the lids.

Patterned Paper and Gift Tags

YOU WILL NEED

Sheets of pale coloured paper

Scrap paper

White candle

Purple, orange and pink acrylic paint

Jam jar

Wide brush

There are so many ways in which to decorate paper. Here is one of the simplest methods. The pattern is created by drawing on the paper with a candle. When the paper is washed over with a strong colour, the paint avoids areas where the wax has been applied, thus leaving a lighter area in the form of the pattern.

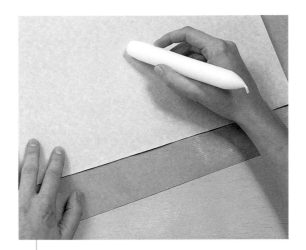

1 Lay the paper to be decorated on a smooth piece of scrap paper to protect the work surface. Draw your design on the paper by pressing really hard with the candle — this is easiest when the candle is cold.

2 Dilute the acrylic paint with water until it has the consistency of light cream. Brush the paint evenly across the surface of the paper to reveal the wax pattern. Lay the paper aside until the paint is dry.

3 Cut out simple shapes from the patterned paper and stick them onto pieces of contrasting-coloured card to make co-ordinating tags. Here the card has been trimmed with pinking shears to make a decorative edge.

Christmas Bird Gift Tags

YOU WILL NEED

❧

Coloured origami paper

❧

Template (see page 155)

❧

Pencil

❧

Small scissors

❧

Scraps of coloured hand-made thick paper

❧

Paper glue

❧

Chinese New Year 'money'

❧

Pinking shears

❧

Hole punch

❧

Short lengths of narrow ribbon

It is extremely rewarding to make your own gift tags at Christmas and it is easy to create beautiful examples with the smallest scraps of paper left over from other projects. Success depends on combining materials with contrasting colours and interesting patterns. Brightly coloured papercut designs, most often of elements from nature, are highly popular in Polish peasant art. You may also like to illustrate the theme from a traditional Christmas carol, such as 'The Twelve Days of Christmas.'

1 Draw around the bird template on a piece of pink origami paper and cut it out. Cut out a background slightly larger than the bird from coloured hand-made paper. Stick the bird into the centre with the paper glue and cut out freehand a crown and wings from the gold part of the Chinese 'money'. Stick in place.

2 Now cut a strip of the same paper the width of the card and trim the top edge with the pinking shears. Stick this along the bottom so it just covers the bird's feet.

3 Cut around the whole tag with pinking shears, keeping the bird centrally placed. Make a hole in one corner with the hole punch and thread with a pretty ribbon.

Christmas Gift Baskets

Basket-making is one of the most ancient and universal crafts. Although baskets were primarily made as purely functional objects, their materials, weaving patterns and eventual shape mean that they are some of the most beautiful examples of human creativity and ingenuity.

YOU WILL NEED

Scrap paper (here sand-coloured soft cotton rag paper and patterned wallpaper were used)

Small stapler

White glue

Small scissors

Paper clips

Mattress needle or needle with wide eye

Paper cord

Pinking shears

Two clothes pegs

1 Cut seven strips of the plain scrap paper, each approximately 30cm (12in) long and 2cm (¾in) wide. Lay them down on the worksurface and weave together as shown, laying three strips across four to form the rectangular base of the basket.

2 Staple each of the four corners to hold the base firmly in place before building up the sides.

3 Bend up all the strips to create the basic structure of the basket. Cut lengths from the patterned paper with the same measurements as before and weave the first layer alternately over and under the upright strips, gluing the beginning and end of each horizontal strip to hold it in place.

6 Use the needle to pierce holes in the woven section of the basket just below the rim and thread the paper cord through and over the rim. Finish off neatly and stick the end of the cord inside with white glue to secure.

4 Continue weaving until four layers are in place, then cut off the excess vertical strips using the small scissors.

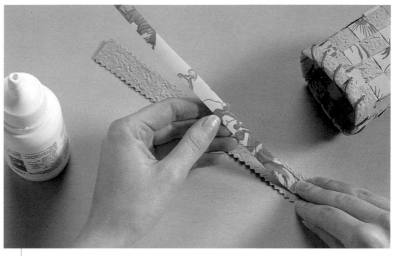

7 Cut a strip of the plain paper 2cm (¾in) wide and 22cm (8¾in) long. Cut each side with the pinking shears to make a pretty zigzagged edge. Stick a strip of the patterned paper 1cm (½in) wide along the centre to make the handle.

5 Cut a length of the plain paper 2cm (¾in) wide and long enough to go around the rim of the basket with a small overlap. Fold it in half lengthways and fit over the rim as shown, holding temporarily in place with paper clips.

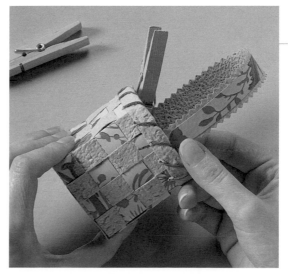

8 Glue each end inside the basket and hold in place with clothes pegs until the glue is completely dry and the handle firmly attached.

Glove Gift Tags

YOU WILL NEED

Templates (see page 155)

Hand-made ivory paper

Paper clips

Pencil

Small pointed scissors

Recycled pink paper

Pinking shears

Wad of tissue paper

Tracing wheel (in two sizes)

Craft knife

Cutting mat

Rubber

Paper glue

Length of ribbon

Hole punch

These subtle and elegant glove-shaped gift tags have been inspired by American folk art designs from the mid-nineteenth century. The heart was a favourite image used to symbolise enduring friendship. The hand or glove design is extremely apt to use as a gift tag due to its connotations of friendship and generosity.

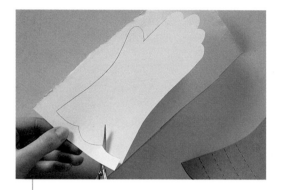

1 Place the template on the ivory-coloured paper and hold in place with paper clips. Draw around it with the pencil, remove the template and cut around the glove shape with the small scissors

3 Place the glove shape on a wad of tissue paper to act as a yielding surface. Using the smaller tracing wheel, press firmly while wheeling it all around the edge of the glove. Make two parallel lines between each finger.

2 Fold the pink paper in half and place the straight side of the heart template against the fold. Cut out the heart plus the two curved strips, also using the template provided. Cut a zigzagged edge with the pinking shears along each edge of the strips.

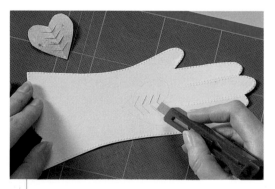

4 Open up the pink heart and lay it on the glove with the point facing the cuff end. Lightly draw around it with a sharp pencil. Now cut four parallel v-shaped slits into the heart and in the heart shape on the back of the glove. Each arm of the slits should measure 1cm (½in).

5 Rub out the pencil marks on the glove. Take the heart, now with its pointed end facing the fingers and carefully interlock the points of the corresponding slits. The heart is now securely fixed onto the glove.

6 Place the curved template onto the cuff of the back of the glove and draw two sets of parallel lines. Place the glove onto the cutting mat and cut twelve slits on the outer band between these lines and ten slits on the inner one.

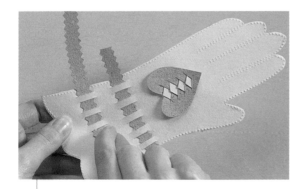

7 Turn the glove over to the right side and slot the pinked strips through the slits. Trim the ends so that 1cm (½in) overlaps, turn under to the back of the glove and stick down with paper glue.

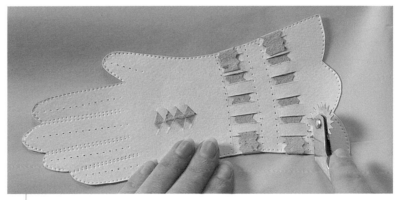

8 Still working from the wrong side, place the glove on the tissue paper and using the larger tracing wheel, mark each side of the strips on the cuff and along the centre of each finger and the thumb. To attach a ribbon, punch a hole at the edge of the cuff.

Crown Cards

YOU WILL NEED

Metallic foil papers

Template (see page 156)

Pencil

Scissors

Wad of folded tissue paper

Sewing tracing wheel

*Red card 30 x 20cm
(12 x 8in)*

*Coloured origami paper 10 x 15cm
(4 x 6in)*

These clever crowns have an 'embossed' design that can be created very easily, but looks very impressive. You can either use the design given on the template for this project or create your own crown motifs.

1 Cut out a piece of the metallic foil paper (handle it very carefully as it marks easily) and place the crown template onto the wrong side. Draw round it neatly with the pencil and cut out.

2 Still working on the back, mark the design on the foil paper with a pencil. Place the foil paper on the wad of folded tissue paper and roll the tracing wheel over the pencil guidelines. This will appear on the metallic side as raised dotted lines which catch the light beautifully.

3 Fold the red card carefully in half, scoring along the fold line. Using the spray glue, stick the red and orange origami paper very neatly in place, butting up to each other in the centre of the card. Finally, spray the back of the crown design and stick centrally over the two-tone background.

Advent Tags

The backing card for these tags is red but you could also use Christmas paper, as long as it is fairly stiff. You can hang these colourful tags on presents as an alternative to a card, or they can go on the boughs of a Christmas tree.

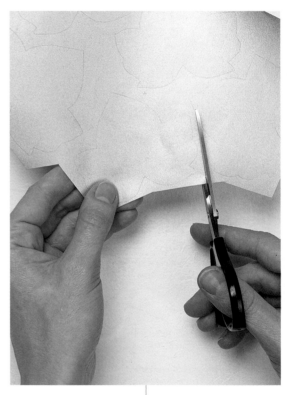

1 Using the template from page 156, draw twenty-four shapes onto the gold paper.

2 Roughly cut out the shapes so that you can tell approximately how large they will be when the tags are finished.

3 Using the scalpel and a template, on each tag cut out the door on three sides.

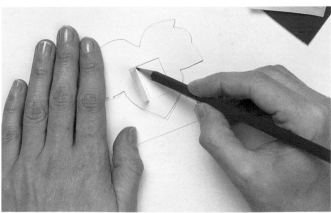

4 | For the backs, draw around the template twenty-four times onto the red card and cut out roughly. On the reverse side of the card, mark where the doors are to go with the pencil and template.

Cathedral Windows

YOU WILL NEED

Red fabric

Needle

Thread

Pins

Tiny beads

Cathedral windows are often used in quilt making and they add a real craft textile touch to a Christmas card. It is always nice to give a card that has the quality of a gift, however small the decoration.

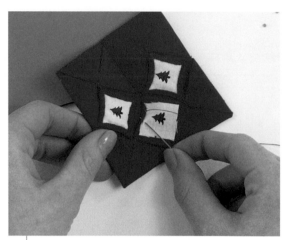

1 Draw four 99cm (3⅛in) squares and cut out. Fold in 6mm (¼in) seam allowance and press. Find square centre by folding diagonally each way and mark with iron tip. Fold down corner and pin. Continue with others to make a square. Catch centre points with a small stitch. Fold in again and sew.

3 Sew double squares together and place the third and fourth fir-tree patches over seams. Sew tiny beads in corners of 'windows'. Cut card 25 x 18cm (10 x 7in), score and fold 12.5cm (5in). Mark top centre and sides 6cm (2⅜in) down with pencil. Cut through card to form a point. Glue finished square centred horizontally onto card. Add gold border.

2 Cut four 2cm (¾in) squares from fir-tree fabric. Place two red squares right sides together and sew down one side to make double square. Pin fir-tree patch diagonally over seam on right side and curl back folded edges surrounding patch. Slip stitch to hold in place. Repeat to make 1 more.

Christmas Stocking Card

YOU WILL NEED

All-purpose adhesive

Silver pen

Red felt

Water soluble pen

Scissors

Felt tip pens

Sequin waste

Sequin waste is a very useful craft material and is used here to make stockings for cards on which any small gifts can be fixed. In this example a small eraser has been used, but you could also attach candies in colourful wrappers or perhaps a small photograph.

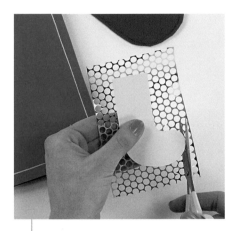

1 Cut card 18 x 23cm (7 x 9in). Score and fold 11.5cm (4½in). Draw border in silver pen around card. Trace the template and transfer onto thin card. Draw round template onto red felt using a water-soluble pen. It is not easy to mark sequin waste so hold the template in place and cut round it.

3 Glue the stocking to card, then add the little pony eraser or another small gift that can be glued on. Draw holly and berries using felt pens. You could also add beads and sequins if you wish.

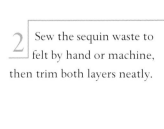

2 Sew the sequin waste to felt by hand or machine, then trim both layers neatly.

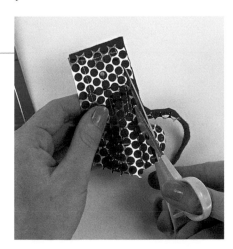

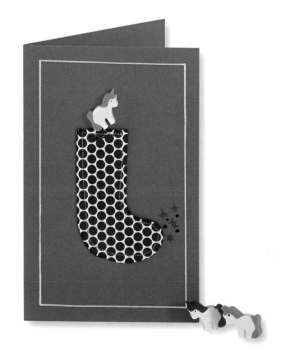

Candlelit Tree

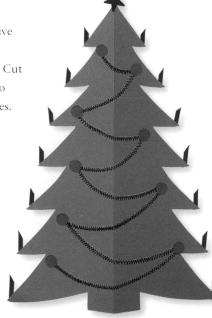
This attractive tree card could also be used as a decoration in its own right. Simply punch a hole though the top of the tree beneath the gold star and thread some strong nylon thread through in a loop to hang from your tree.

1 Cut card 15 x 20cm (6 x 8in) and score down centre. Trace template and transfer onto thin card and draw round on green card. Cut out using craft knife. Set your sewing machine to a fairly wide satin stitch.

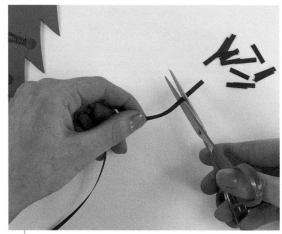

3 Glue the ribbon pieces in place at the end of branches on the back of the card. Tweezers will help you to hold them steady. Leave until the glue dries. Cut the tops diagonally to look like candles. Add a red star on top of the tree.

2 Stick on self-adhesive spots to resemble Christmas tree baubles. Cut narrow satin ribbon into fourteen 1cm (½in) pieces.

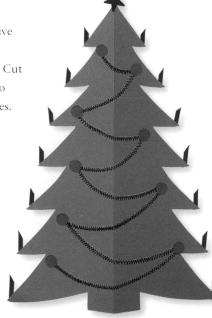

The Friendly Snowman Card

The snowman at the window invites us to come outside to play in the snow. This is such a pretty card, why not decorate it with surrounding 'drifts' of absorbent cotton balls displayed somewhere where your card can be seen?

YOU WILL NEED

Coloured card

Piece of film

Paper

Pencil

Chinagraph pencils

Silver pen

Double-sided tape

1 | Cut off left hand side of this card so that light will shine through window. Cut a piece of film slightly smaller than folded card. Draw snowman and trees on to the paper Place paper under film and on right side draw outline of snowman and trees.

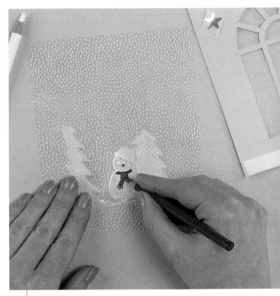

3 | Turn back the film onto the right side and draw in the scarf and nose with a red chinagraph pencil. Add face details in silver. Attach the film to the inside of card with double-sided tape and place a silver star where it can be seen shining through window.

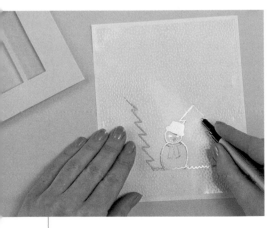

2 | Turn over the film and colour in the trees and snowman using a white chinagraph pencil.

A Christmas Fir Tree Card

YOU WILL NEED

White card

Green plastic strips

Orange and yellow tissue paper

Self-adhesive

Spray glue

Steel ruler

Sharp craft knife

This is a simple, easily-made card in unusual colours for Christmas. You can recycle old colourful plastic bags for this project as these make a durable material with an interesting texture.

1 Cut card 11 x 20cm (4¼ x 8in), score and fold 10cm (4in). The fold is at the top of card. Cut a strip of green plastic from an old shopping bag. Tear four strips of tissue in shades of orange and yellow. The fir-tree is from a strip of self-adhesive 'stickers'.

3 Trim excess paper from the edges of the card with a steel ruler and sharp craft knife.

2 Arrange the strips so that colours overlap and produce new colours and tones. Stick down the tree. Spray glue onto the back of strips and stick down.

Paper Holly Christmas Card

YOU WILL NEED

❧

Silver card

❧

Scissors

❧

Thin card for templates

❧

Dark and light-green satin paper

❧

Spray glue

❧

Self-adhesive red spots

The silver card shows off the greens and reds of the holly to stunning effect in this simple design. You will need to buy some satin paper from a craft shop to use for the glossy leaves.

1 Cut silver card 30 x 15cm (12 x 6in), score and fold 15cm (6in). Trace templates and transfer onto card.

2 Cut 13cm (5in) square of satin paper and 10cm (4in) square of dark green tissue-paper. Fold these squares in half twice, then diagonally across to make a triangle. Cut out larger holly from satin paper and unfold, then dark green holly. You can draw round templates first if you find it easier.

3 Spray glue onto the backs of holly leaves. Position the larger, pale-green leaves first, then the dark green on top, between the pale-green leaves. Stationer's self-adhesive spots make red berries. Put on five or so.

Curled Ribbon Tree Card

This clever card is made using sequin waste and colorful ribbons in a truly ingenious way. This would also make a good wedding or christening card as the curled ribbons add a celebratory touch – you can simply cut out appropriate shapes for the occasion and thread the ribbons through.

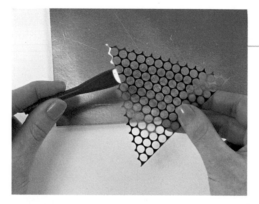

1 Cut card 15 x 22cm (6 x 8½in), score and fold 11cm (4¼in) along the top. Mark centre top of the card with the pencil dot. Cut the triangle from sequin waste, place on the card and mark two sides at the bottom of the tree. Glue along edges of tree and hold in place on card until the glue dries. Any residue glue can be rubbed away when it is dry.

2 Cut a base for the tree from a piece of card or paper. Curl over scissors a number of narrow pieces of ribbon cut about 9.5cm (3¾in) long.

3 Glue on base and add sequin star to top of tree. Slip curled ribbons through every other hole in sequin waste and every other row, starting at top of tree. There is no need to tie them; they will stay in place.

New Year Dove Card

YOU WILL NEED

Deep-blue card

Pencil

Craft knife

Tracing paper

Template (see page 156)

White paper doily

Old calendar

Translucent film

Spray glue

4 star sequins

Silver pen

This dove of peace for New Year is made from a paper doily with calendar dates falling from its beak. Once the festivities are over and you find yourself looking forward to a new year, send this card to friends and congratulate them on surviving Christmas!

1 | Cut deep blue card 30 x 20cm (12 x 8in), score 15cm (6in) and fold. Draw freehand two curves at the top of the card to represent clouds and cut with a craft knife.

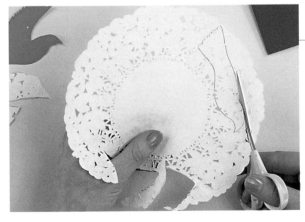

2 | Trace the dove template and transfer to thin card to make your own template. Trace out the dove onto white paper doily and cut out, together with dates 1 and 31 from an old calendar and the strip of translucent film waved along the upper edge to resemble hills.

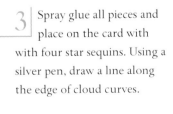

3 | Spray glue all pieces and place on the card with with four star sequins. Using a silver pen, draw a line along the edge of cloud curves.

Food Gifts

Amaretto Wrappers

YOU WILL NEED

Template (see page 157)

Stencil card cut to the size of the finished wrappers

Pencil

Scalpel or craft knife

Cutting mat

Tissue paper

Pebbles

Gold spray paint

Rough paper

Organza ribbon

If the tissue paper ends up being slightly larger than the stencil, don't worry: it will have a lovely golden edge in addition to the golden stencil.

1 Using the templates on page 157 or one of your own (perhaps copy a design from a Christmas card or paper), transfer the design onto stencil card. Simple geometric designs work best.

3 Cut pieces of tissue paper to the same size as the card. Lay the card over the tissue paper, on rough paper to protect your worksurface and use pebbles to hold it in place. Lightly spray with gold spray paint.

2 On a cutting mat, carefully cut out the design with the scalpel or craft knife.

4 When the paint is dry, wrap each biscuit or sweet in a stenciled paper and tie the ends with organza ribbon.

Aniseed Biscuits

YOU WILL NEED

INGREDIENTS

4 eggs

500g (1lb 1½oz) icing sugar

500g (1lb 1½oz) white flour

20ml (2 dessertspoons) aniseed

EQUIPMENT

Baking tray

Rolling pin

Biscuit moulds

Sharp knife

Aniseed biscuits are traditionally baked at Christmas in Switzerland and Germany, where exquisite examples can be bought from good bakers' shops. They are often given as presents and, rather than being eaten, are hung on the wall as decorations.

1 Beat the eggs together with the icing sugar until light and fluffy, using an electric whisk if you have one. Mix in the flour and gradually add the aniseed. Turn out the mixture onto a lightly floured surface and knead very lightly. Roll out the dough to a thickness of approximately 1cm (½in).

3 Press the mould firmly and evenly down onto the dough to transfer the image. Lift off carefully and place the biscuit on a very lightly greased baking tray.

2 Lay the mould gently on the dough and, without pressing, cut around the mould to release a piece of dough the same size as the mould.

4 Using the larger composite mould, press firmly and evenly onto the pastry. Remove the mould and cut the shapes into smaller biscuits. Place on the lightly greased baking tray and leave to dry overnight. Bake low down in an oven preheated to 140°C/275°F/gas mark 1 for approximately 35 minutes or until biscuits have risen and formed a base and top layer.

Gingerbread House

YOU WILL NEED

INGREDIENTS

100g (4oz) butter

200g (7oz) black treacle

175g (6oz) honey

500g (1lb 1½oz) all-purpose white flour

100g (4oz) ground almonds

15ml (1 tbsp) ground ginger

5ml (1 tsp) mixed spice

5ml (1 tsp) cinnamon

2.5ml (½ tsp) nutmeg

10ml (2 tsp) bicarbonate of soda

100g (4oz) chopped preserved ginger

100g (4oz) chopped mixed peel

You will need to make 3 times this amount for the house shown here.

ROYAL ICING

500g (1lb 1½oz) Icing sugar

Whites of 2 large eggs

5ml (1 tsp) lemon juice

EQUIPMENT

Rolling pin

2 baking trays

Small kitchen knife

Piping bag and nozzles

Cake board 23 x 33cm (9 x 13in)

This is an elegant adaptation of the more homely German tradition of making a Lebkuchen Haus at Christmas. These confectionery masterpieces were generally more in the style of a Hansel and Gretel-type cottage, freely decorated with drifts of icing snow and lavishly adorned with brightly coloured sweets and enticing biscuits.

1 Warm the butter, treacle and honey in a pan until blended, then cool a little. In a bowl mix together the dry ingredients, chopped ginger and peel. Add the cooled butter mixture to the dry ingredients. Mix together, turn onto a floured surface and knead lightly. Add a little milk if the dough is too dry or a little flour if too wet. Roll out onto the greased baking tray to a thickness of 1cm (½in).

2 Lay your house template on the pastry and cut around it. Repeat for the sides and roof pieces. The back is cut from the front template without cutting out the windows and door. Preheat the oven to 200°C/400°F/gas mark 6 and bake for about 20 minutes until a rich brown colour. Allow to cool, then remove from the tray. If the gingerbread has spread, replace the template and cut around once more.

3 | Beat the egg whites until frothy and slowly add the sifted sugar and lemon juice, beating until it holds up in peaks. Fill the icing bag and use the smallest nozzle to pipe around the windows and door. Pipe a double line around the front and fill in with dots. Pipe a border along the bottom and add dots and stars. Decorate the sides as shown.

4 | Pipe the design onto the roof pieces – a crossed border along the top with a latticework design on the main section. To finish, pipe a dot into each diamond. The back of the house need not be decorated as it will not be seen.

5 | To make the icing glue, beat the remaining royal icing mixture until it becomes much thicker. Fill the piping bag and insert a larger nozzle. Pipe a generous amount of the icing along the size and back of the cake board. Pipe another line up the side of the back wall where it will join the side wall. Place the back and side on the icing glue and push the side against the back, making sure that they both stand upright.

6 Continue in this manner adding the other side and front. The icing glue is very strong and should hold the pieces together well when it sets. Pipe along the top of the roof and along the front edges of the gable end. Carefully put the front section of the roof on the house and press it gently into place. Repeat to attach the back section.

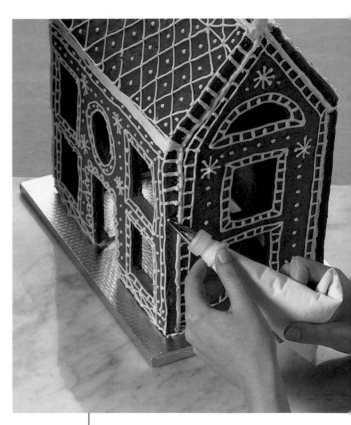

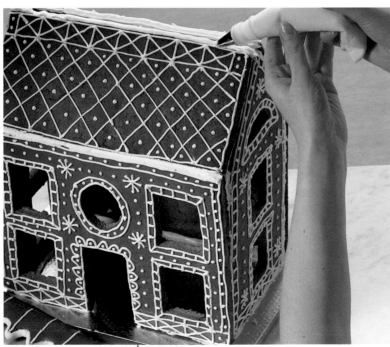

7 When the two roof sections are in place, a small gap will be left between them at the top. Pipe along both edges of this gap and fix the roof ridge in place.

8 Clean away any icing glue that oozes out of the joins from under the base of the house with the kitchen knife. Replace the narrow nozzle on the bag and, using the original icing mixture, disguise the joins by piping into them as well as piping horizontal lines up the sides, the front and roof.

Chocolate Snowflake Stars

YOU WILL NEED

INGREDIENTS

200g (7oz) dark chocolate

225g (8oz) butter, softened

225g (8oz) fine granulated sugar

3 eggs

Pinch of salt

500g (1lb 1½oz) flour

ROYAL ICING

500g (1lb 1½oz) icing sugar

Whites of 2 large eggs

5ml (1 tsp) lemon juice

EQUIPMENT

Rolling pin

Baking tray

Star-shaped biscuit cutter

Icing bag and nozzle

Simple to make and decorated using the enduring wintry theme of snowflakes, these delicious star-shaped biscuits will appeal to children – in fact they could be made by children who love to stamp out interesting shapes with tin biscuit cutters. These can be found in many different shapes and sizes in good kitchen supply stores.

1 Melt the chocolate, add to the softened butter and mix. In another bowl beat the sugar and eggs together, add a pinch of salt and the flour. Stir in the chocolate mixture. Turn out onto a floured surface and knead lightly, then roll out the pastry to a thickness of 5mm (2½in).

3 Sift the icing sugar. Beat the egg whites until just frothy and slowly add the sifted sugar and the lemon juice, beating all the time until the icing stands up in peaks. Fill the icing bag and, using the finest nozzle, pipe a star shape onto the biscuits. The icing must be just the right consistency to make good clean lines – if it is too runny it will spread; too stiff and it will not adhere to the biscuit when set.

2 Cut out the star shapes with the biscuit cutter and place them carefully on a baking tray. Preheat the oven to 200°C/400°F/gas mark 6 and bake for 10 minutes. Remove from oven and allow to cool.

4 Now pipe radiating lines from the simple star shape to form a snowflake. When the icing has set, store in an airtight tin.

Meringue Mice

YOU WILL NEED

*4 egg whites
(at room temperature)*

*225g (8oz)
fine granulated sugar*

Baking tray

Waxproof paper

Piping bag

Palette knife

Edible silver balls

Peppercorns

Split almonds

Bradawl

Gold wire string

PREPARATION

*Place the egg whites
in a large bowl and whisk at high
speed until soft peaks form. Add
the sugar, 1 tsp at a
time, whisking well
each time.*

Meringue is best cooked at a low temperature for two hours so make sure you have plenty of time ahead of you. This recipe makes about sixteen mice.

1 Line the baking tray with waxproof paper and heat the oven to 100°C/225°F/ gas mark ¼. Then spoon the mixture into a piping bag and squeeze wedge shapes on the waxproof paper.

2 Smooth the shapes into small mice-like bodies using the palette knife. Keep back some of the meringue for step 4.

3 To make the mice faces, add silver balls for the noses, peppercorns for the eyes (don't forget to remove these before eating!) and split almonds for the ears.

4 Bake in the oven for about two hours or until very slightly golden. Cool and then use the bradawl to poke a small hole for the tail. Add the gold wire string for the tail, fastening it with uncooked meringue.

Festive Cookies

YOU WILL NEED

110g (4oz) butter

50g (2oz) fine granulated sugar

Grated rind of one lemon

150g (5oz) all-purpose flour

Rolling pin

Variety of cutters

Wax paper

Baking tray

Edible silver balls

Bradawl

Silver string

Edible silver balls are very attractive decorations and can be used for all sorts of patterns and pictures on these pretty biscuits.

1 | Mix all the ingredients together in a mixer. Heat the oven to 180°C/240°F/gas mark 4 and roll out the pastry on a floured surface.

2 | Cut out a variety of shapes using the biscuit cutters. Try to cut as many as possible from the pastry so that you don't have to roll it out too frequently.

3 | Lay the biscuits on a piece of waxproof paper on a baking tray and decorate with the edible silver balls.

4 Make a hole in each biscuit with the bradawl before putting them in the oven for 10 minutes until pale brown. Once cooked, cool on a wire rack and thread the holes with silver string to hang.

Christmas Tree Treats

YOU WILL NEED

Variety of cutters

Greased baking sheet

Icing sugar

Water

Waxed thread or ribbon

These edible decorations are ideal for children to make and give to their friends or teachers. Make the biscuits following a basic recipe using sugar, eggs, flour and butter in the usual proportions.

1 Cut the dough into festive shapes. Skewer a hole in each, so that you can push a thread through later. (This may close up during baking – in which case you will have to pierce another hole in them when they are cold – but very carefully, as the biscuits have a habit of breaking!) Put them onto a greased baking sheet and bake them at 180°C/350°F/gas mark 4, for 15 minutes.

2 When the biscuits are cool, make up some fairly stiff icing using icing sugar and water and ice them. Thread them onto some waxed thread – or ribbon if the hole is big enough.

Almond Bunches

YOU WILL NEED

For each bunch:
2 10cm (4in) squares of net
in contrasting colours

3 sugared almonds

45cm (18in) length of ribbon,
6mm (¼in) wide

A few sugared almonds wrapped in coloured net make a sophisticated-looking tree decoration – with the added bonus that you can give them away to friends and visitors over the festive season.

1 Place the two net squares one on top of the other.

2 Place the three almonds in the centre of the net squares and bring up the corners to form a neat bag.

3 Fold the ribbon in half and make a single stitch about 10cm (4in) from the fold. Hold the ribbon loop behind the almond bunch and tie the loose ends at the front in a bow.

Decorated Biscuits

YOU WILL NEED

❦

BASIC RECIPE

For the biscuits:

75g (3oz) butter

40g (1½oz) fine granulated sugar

25g (1oz) cornstarch

75g (3oz) all-purpose flour

❦

FOR THE WATER ICING

250g (8oz) icing sugar

6 dessertspoons warm water

❦

EQUIPMENT

Drinking straws

Palette knife

Children will enjoy helping to decorate these Christmas biscuits. The biscuits should be eaten within a week of being made — though you probably won't be able to resist them for that long!

1 While still warm, push a short length of a drinking straw into the top of each biscuit shape to make a hole for hanging. Leave the straw in place.

2 Using a palette knife, put a small amount of water icing in the middle of each shape. Working quickly before the biscuits cool, spread the icing evenly over the top and sides. Mix together the icing sugar and water to the consistency of pouring cream.

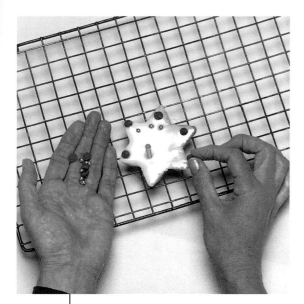

3 Decorate the biscuits with chocolate chips and silver cake decorations. Leave to cool. Store in an airtight container for two days to allow the icing to harden.

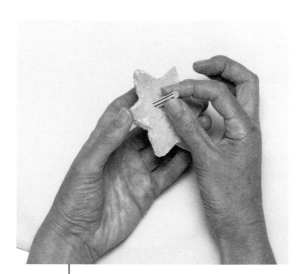

4 Remove the drinking straws by pushing them through the back of the biscuits from the front (if you pull out the straws from the front, you may crack the icing).

5 Fold a ribbon length in half and push the folded end through the hole in the biscuit from the back. Feed the cut ends through the loop and pull tight. Tie the cut ends together to form a loop for hanging and cut off any excess ribbon on the diagonal to neaten.

Piped Chocolate Treats

YOU WILL NEED

Chocolate

Butter

Heavy cream

Yolk of 1 egg

Petit-fours cases

Wax paper

Adhesive tape

Fluted nozzle

An easy and delicious chocolate filling can be quickly whipped up by melting chocolate over a pan of hot water and then stirring in a cube of butter, one egg yolk and a little heavy cream. Beat the mixture and leave it to cool before using to fill meringues, decorate petit-fours, to pipe onto cakes, or to make the cups shown here.

1 Making chocolate cups: To make the filling, melt chocolate over a pan of boiling water and then add butter, cream and egg yolk and beat well.

2 Melt more chocolate and, using a spoon, coat the insides of small petit-fours cases. Allow to set, then apply a second coat.

3 Place the cases in a cool place to allow the second coat of chocolate to set, then peel away the cases to reveal the chocolate 'cups'.

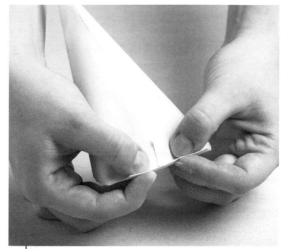

6 Turn in the corners at the open end of the cone and crease to secure. A paper clip or adhesive tape will keep them in place.

4 Making a piping bag: Make a 25 x 10cm (10 x 4in) rectangle from waxproof paper. Fold the paper diagonally in half to form two triangular shapes.

5 Fold the blunt end of the triangle to create a pointed cone. Bring over the other end, making the pointed as possible.

7 Fit a fluted nozzle then fill the piping bag with chocolate filling and pipe it into the cases. Decorate as desired.

Templates

Chapter 1: Decorating the Home

COPPER CANDLE SCONCE, PAGE 15

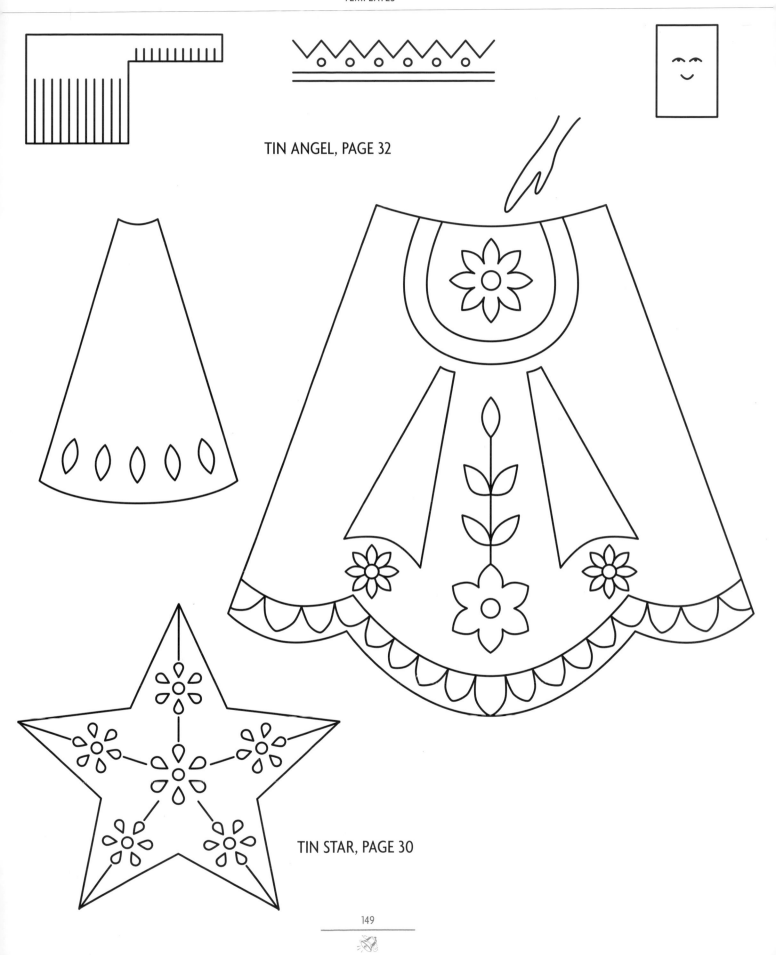

TIN ANGEL, PAGE 32

TIN STAR, PAGE 30

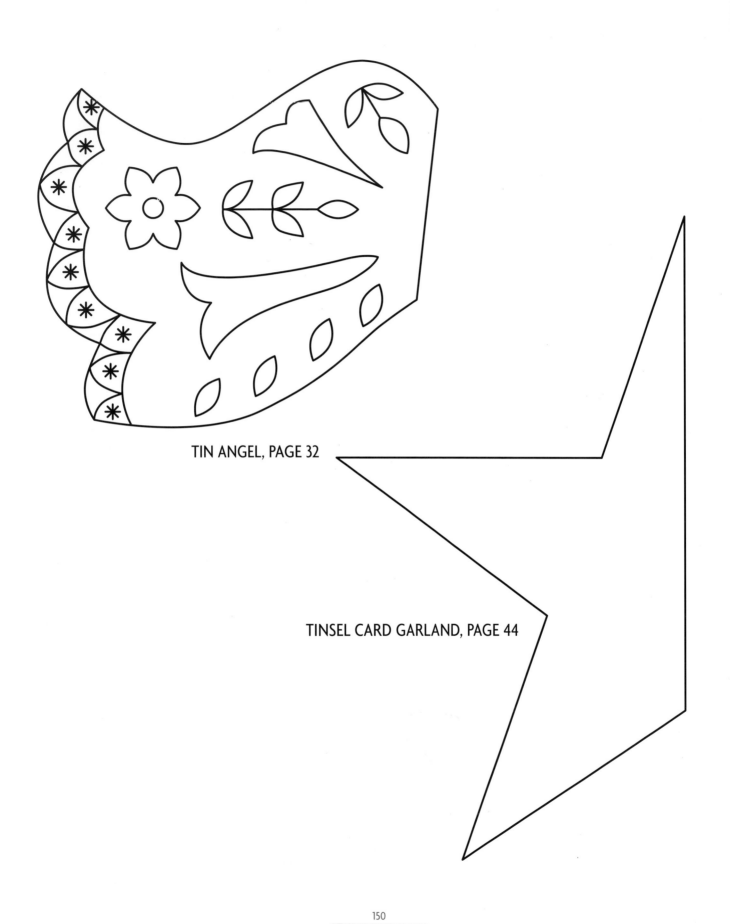

TIN ANGEL, PAGE 32

TINSEL CARD GARLAND, PAGE 44

BEADED RAINBOW CATCHER DESIGNS,
PAGE 48. ENLARGE TO 200%

Chapter 2: Decorating the Tree

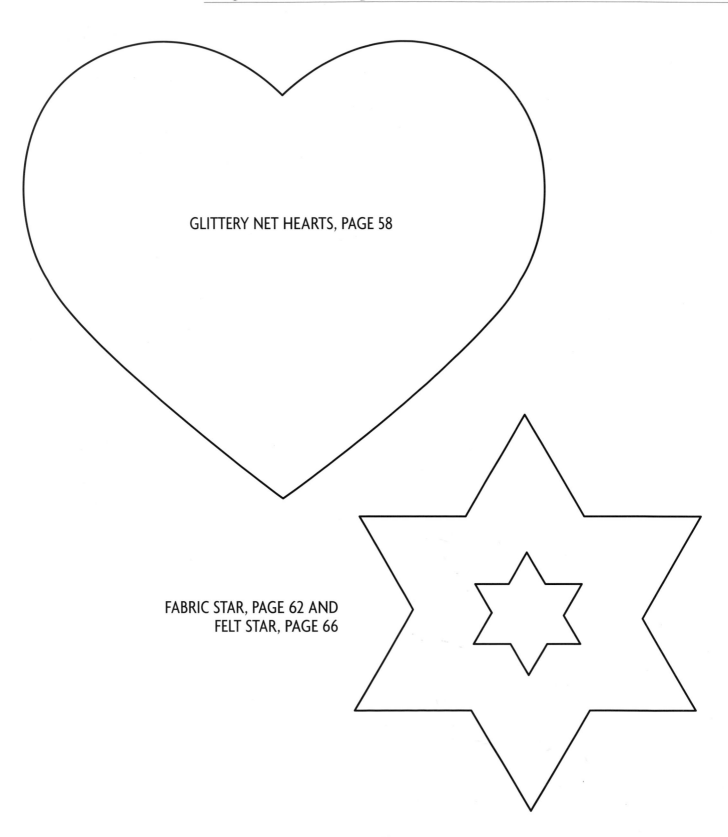

GLITTERY NET HEARTS, PAGE 58

FABRIC STAR, PAGE 62 AND
FELT STAR, PAGE 66

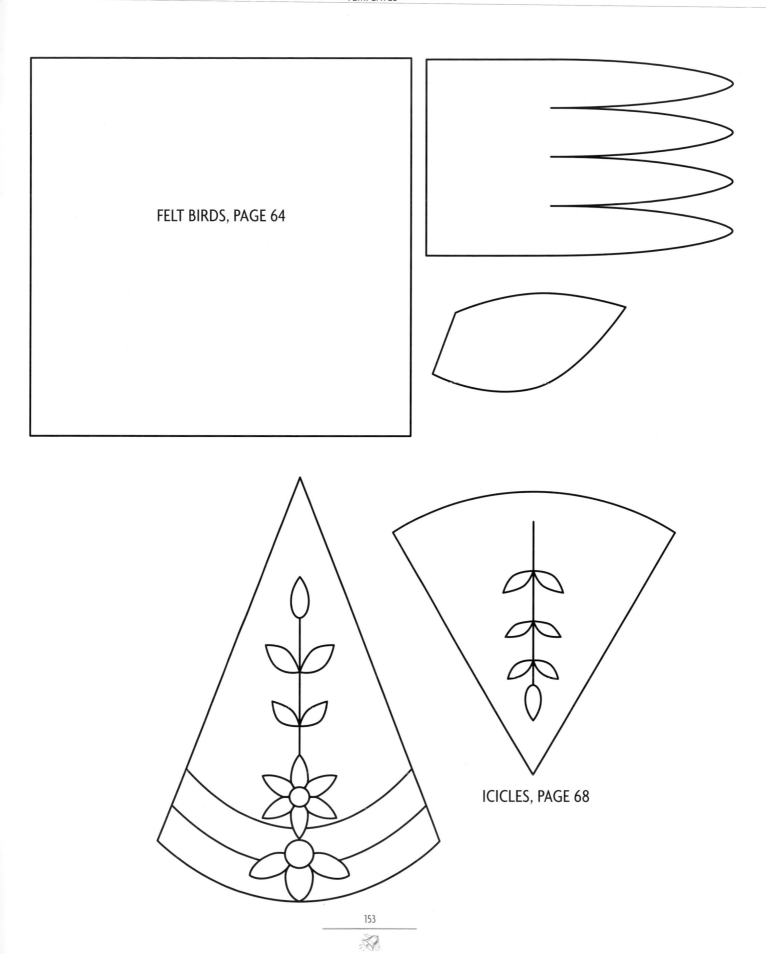

FELT BIRDS, PAGE 64

ICICLES, PAGE 68

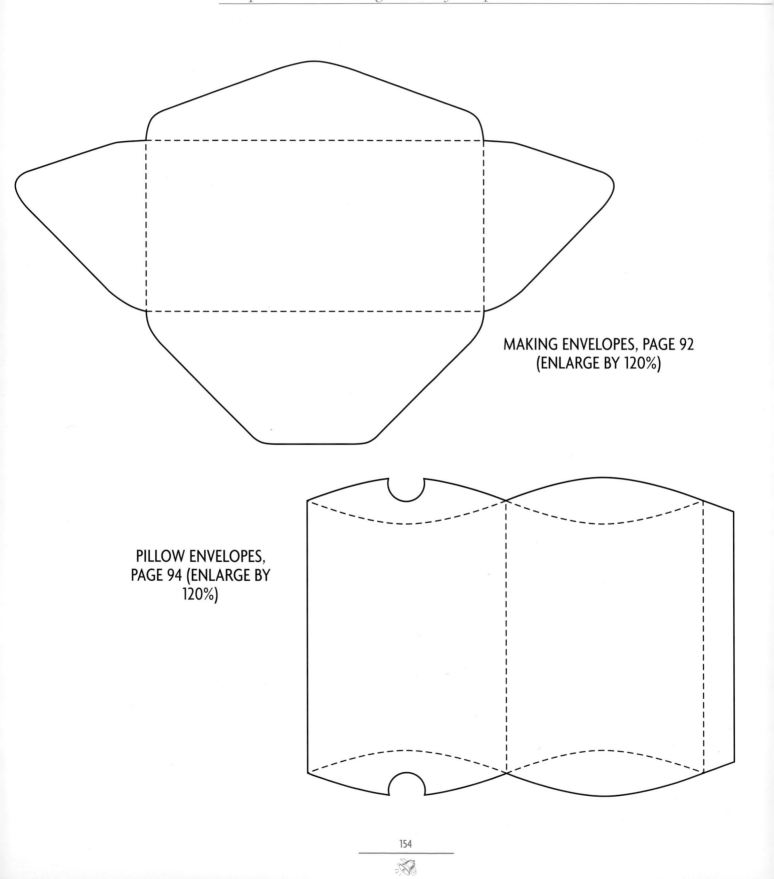

**MAKING ENVELOPES, PAGE 92
(ENLARGE BY 120%)**

**PILLOW ENVELOPES,
PAGE 94 (ENLARGE BY
120%)**

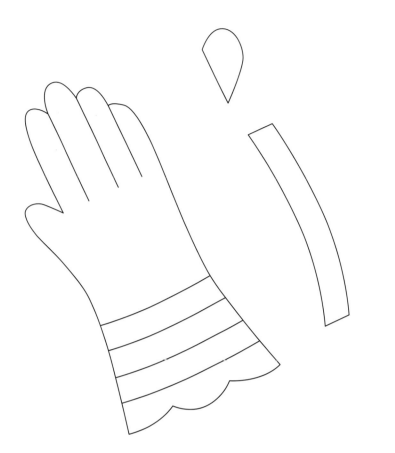

GLOVE GIFT TAGS, PAGE 112 (ENLARGE BY 200%)

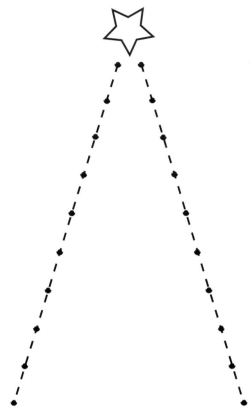

COLOURFUL CHRISTMAS, PAGE 96

BIRD FELT GIFT TAGS,
PAGE 108

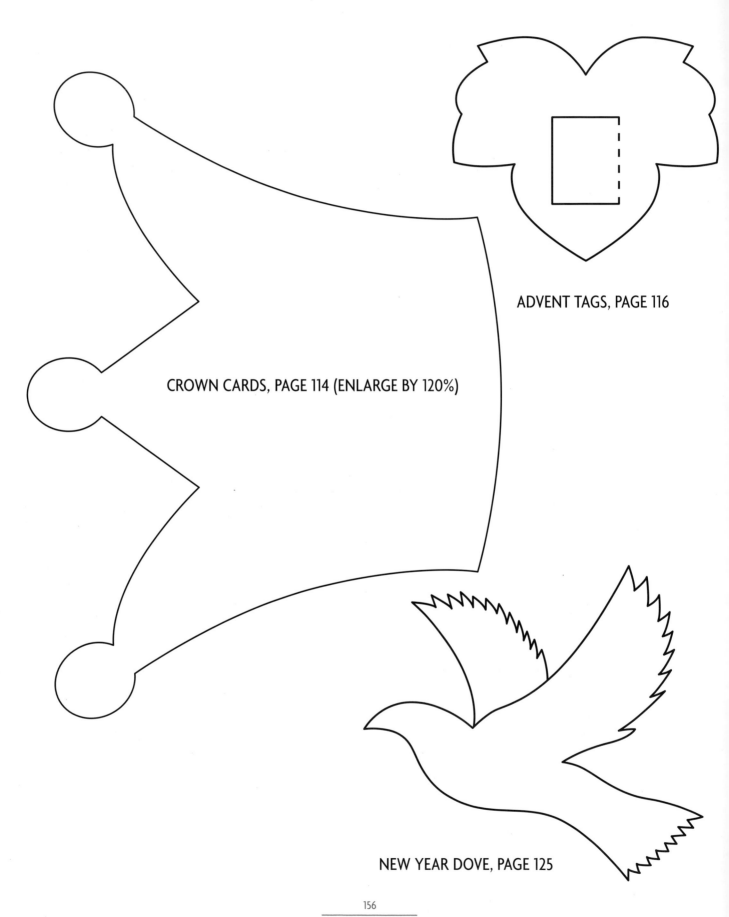

ADVENT TAGS, PAGE 116

CROWN CARDS, PAGE 114 (ENLARGE BY 120%)

NEW YEAR DOVE, PAGE 125

Chapter 4: Food Gifts

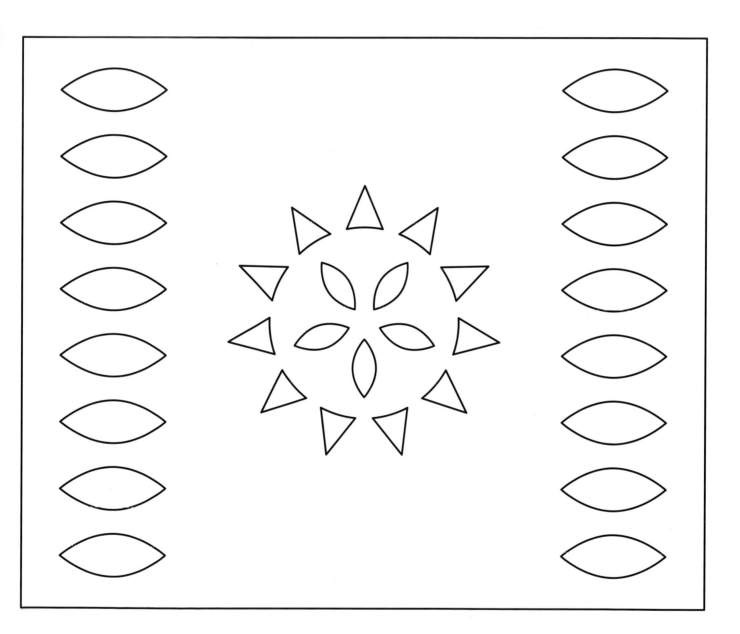

AMARETTO WRAPPERS, PAGE 128

Index

Acknowledgments

Alan and Barry would like to thank all the

contributors whose projects have been featured in

this book, notably Claire Leavey, Carol

McCleeve, Stephanie Donaldson, Simon Lycett,

Deborah Schneebeli-Morrell, and Sarah

Beaman. They would also like to thank Miranda

Sessions, Marie Clayton, and Katie Cowan at

Collins & Brown for their enthusiasm and

support in putting this book together.

Thanks one and all.